Louis Aragon
Jean Cocteau

Conversations on the
Dresden Gallery

Louis Aragon/ Jean Cocteau

Conversations on the Dresden Gallery

Translated from the French by Francis Scarfe

Foreword by Joseph Masheck

HM

Holmes & Meier
Publishers
New York · London

First published in the United States of America 1982 by
Holmes & Meier Publishers, Inc.
30 Irving Place, New York, N.Y. 10003

Great Britain:
Holmes & Meier Publishers, Ltd.
131 Trafalgar Road, Greenwich, London SE10 9TX

Originally published in French as *Entretiens sur le Musée de Dresde*
© Editions Cercle d'Art, Paris, 1957
English translation © 1982 by Edition Leipzig
Foreword © 1982 by Holmes & Meier Publishers, Inc.
ALL RIGHTS RESERVED

Library of Congress Cataloging in Publication Data
Aragon, 1897–
    European masters of the Dresden Gallery
    Translation of: Entretiens sur le Musée de Dresde.
    1. Gemäldegalerie Dresden.   I. Cocteau, Jean, 1889–
1963.   II. Gemäldegalerie Dresden.   III. Title.
N2280.A9413   759.94'074'0321   81–6640
ISBN 0-8419-0730-7   AACR2

Design: Ulrike Weissgerber
Manufactured in the German Democratic Republic

Contents

Foreword

"Communist meets esthete" might suggest a squabble, but Louis Aragon and Jean Cocteau, two great individualists who had shunned each other for years, are amply cordial in these free-form dialogues occasioned by the reopening of the Dresden Gemäldegalerie after the war, celebrating at the same time their reconciliation. Having picked out reproductions (evidently postcards and slides), both soon enough realized that they had chosen many of the same paintings. The discussions themselves show the possibility, or even the (Surrealist) necessity, of arriving at the truth by means of one's individual humanity.

Descriptive, "pictures-at-an-exhibition" tours like this belong to a genre that includes private, diaristic responses; belles-lettristric obser-vations in which the reader is invited vicariously to share; and the most public criticism, as of official Salons. Even the critical gallery tour of past masterpieces has its modern history, including a series of "Musées d'Europe" picture books with running commentary by the Symbolist critic Geffroy and, pertinently for Aragon and Cocteau's appreciation of Flemish and German painting, art writings by J. K. Huysmans. We should recall also the still closer precedent of the "imaginary museum" or "museum without walls" of André Malraux (1951). Later, Pierre Schneider's *Louvre Dialogues* with contemporary French and American artists, begun in the 1960s, are also noteworthy; indeed, the emergence of the New York School, as a threat to the 300-year hegemony of Paris, conceivably generates some unspoken anxiety over pure abstract peint-ing in these Aragon—Cocteau dialogues of 1956.

Dialogues themselves are of various types: the fictional drama of speculation; the interview by an interlocutor figure on the reader's behalf; and the conversation between high equals, as here. Aragon and Cocteau entertain themselves, one another, and us with a luxuriously casual, sportive play of ideas. They seem not so much to sit face to face as side by side, mutually trading responses to each mute but vividly apprehended work, sometimes in reciprocally interrupted monologues. Actually, when they compare black-and-white photographs and color slides of the same paintings, this may seem apt just because their diver-gent reactions to the same works are already co-present in the reader's mind.

Appropriately, Aragon talks at one point about the history of museums. The Gemäldegalerie, categorically a *Pinakothek*, or picture gallery (to the exclusion of all else), is a distinguished descendant of the "curiosity cabinets" of, especially, the German Renaissance. As such, it is a prime instance in the historic differentiation of art from nature and, later, of the reclassification of all arts and manufactures as *cultural*. The earliest Dresden paintings did belong to a *Kunst- und Wunderkammer* (art and curiosity cabinet) founded in 1560, but by 1720 (even as Linnaeus worked toward the systematic classification of flora and fauna) the collection was being broken down into specialized departments of art and science, notably with precious metalwork kept in the separate "Green Vaults"; in 1835 remaining unclassified objects were auctioned off.

The actual Gemäldegalerie building, built between 1847 and 1854, was designed by Gottfried Semper, who has his own place in museum history. As a wing embracing the courtyard of the old general museum of the Zwinger palace (1711–22), Semper's picture gallery both extended the new idea of fine art in isolation and yet also brought painting into a newly complementary relation with "curiosities." Such was clearly on Semper's mind, since in his concurrent "Plan for an Ideal Museum" (1852), as though compensating for the categorical limitations of the Dresden project, he elaborates the idea of one museum giving equalized systematic emphasis to all arts, with objects classified by their material and structural properties. Semper went on (with Karl von Hasenauer) to build, between 1872 and 1881, the most famous of all mirror pairs of art and natural history museums, the Kunsthistorisches und Natur-historisches Museums of Vienna (other such couples occur elsewhere in the nineteenth century, as in Dublin).

Thanks to the catalog of the "Splendor of Dresden" exhibition shown in Washington, New York, and San Francisco in 1978–79, one can trace the changing museological significance of such a single work admired by both Aragon and Cocteau as Cranach's *Duke Henry the Pious*. This portrait entered the *Kunstkammer* in 1641, on a par with natural specimens of beauty and fascination; in 1838, which is to say in the time of Romantic nationalism, it was moved to the Historical Museum, serving as a document of the Reformation; only in 1905, when the modern concept of intrinsic artistic value was emergent, was it installed in the paintings gallery.

The earlier Northern paintings which Aragon and Cocteau like so much were at first just what happened to be around from the more miscellaneous earlier times. In the eighteenth century, surely as a func-tion of the economic decline of Italy and consequent sales, the Gemälde-galerie gained greatly in Italian works: preeminent is the famous *Dresden* (or *Sistene*) Madonna of Raphael, bought from the church of San Sisto in Piacenza in 1754 — a painting that Aragon and Cocteau pass over, no doubt as a too obvious war-horse. The modern discovery of the Northern "primitives" was affirmed with an exhibition of "Les Primitifs flamands" at Bruges in 1902. Soon even Baedeker's guidebooks would be explaining, of the Dresden collection, "In accordance with the taste prevalent at the time of its foundation, the gallery is somewhat sparingly provided with early works." Hence it is largely to a collection of old masters, in the classical sense, that Aragon and Cocteau turn, though they delight in many exceptions as well as in less familiar works from the mainstream.

Sometimes Picasso seems to hover here. Cocteau stands by him, even against Matisse, though he seems to regret the eclipse by Cubism of a less complex modernity in painting around 1913. Cocteau had become associated with Picasso specifically in regard to the decor for the ballet *Parade*, in 1916—17. Indeed, if the dialogues had taken place earlier, they might have touched on Cocteau's general contentment with surface, not to say superficial, effect, at least from Aragon's point of view. Otherwise, both Aragon and Cocteau consider Picasso's so-called "distortions" of the human image, and, more enlighteningly, his fresh interest in older masters removed from the Raphaelesque tradition of perfectly resolved form, including Cranach.

Cranach, in particular, was problematic for modernity. The young Paul Klee had reversed an earlier distaste before his Florence version of *Adam and Eve*, in 1902, noting with admiration, in a diary entry, the disposition of the figure of Eve. The important critic Julius Meier-Graefe, however, in his influential *Modern Art* (1904), specifically warned against seeing anything like a French beauty in Cranach, no German having ever painted "woman as woman" anyway: "It is mere perversity to extract from Cranach something allied to the French manner." To the early modern Russian theoretician Nikolai Tarabukin, Cranach's portraits seemed, interestingly enough, like still lifes in comparison with the "biographical" portraits of Rembrandt or Velázquez. More contemporaneously, Matisse, in the introduction to his album *Portraits* (1954), finding particularity and asymmetry of the essence in portraiture, praised Cranach, along with Dürer and Holbein, for his very divergence from the classical, Mediterranean generalization of form and structure.

In a biography of Jean Cocteau (1970), Francis Steegmuller claims that "the two poets recorded — it is not clear why — a long and tedious dialogue on the subject of the pictures from the destroyed museum in Dresden." But the texture and flavor of the conversation seems at least as important as the tenor of the discussion, even if sheer French cleverness sometimes rises to inflationary peaks. The very aimlessness of the dialogue seems a matter of unguarded mutual respect, as two profoundly different men overcome a long, and no doubt largely political, estrangement. Each finds his own way back to the less mitigated enthusiasms of their younger days. Integrity had split Aragon and Cocteau apart; the moral seriousness with which they take art, in ways as different as ever, drives them together.

The very literacy of these informal conversations encourages the reader's own awareness, even little mistakes being a matter of the fluency of thought. (In a true Surrealist spirit, Aragon had long before announced in a *Treatise of Style* a refusal even to correct typographical errors, while, for his part, Cocteau apparently liked the present experiment with tape-recording enough to use it subsequently in his writing.) Many single themes might be explored further, for example Cocteau's proto-Pop fascination with the stylized image of a Zouave (Algerian soldier) in the trademark of "Job" cigarette papers. Cocteau always had a Baudelairian taste for such stylistic detail in everyday life, as where, in his autobiography *(Professional Secrets)*, he makes a point of Juan Gris's claim to have introduced the motif of the siphon bottle into Cubist painting.

Cocteau refers to the Surrealists as "your group" because he, a homosexual, had always been unwelcome in the orthodox inner circle presided over by André Breton. But Aragon replies to his suggestion that the Surrealists would have admired Tintoretto's *Deliverance of Arsinoë* with "If only they knew how to look at it," to which Cocteau adds, "You are more royalist than the king." The exchange alludes to Aragon's own eventual heterodox status, vis-à-vis the Breton circle. But if both were mavericks, they also, despite their divergent attitudes, had indeed been closer. Aragon's stance was obvious in his advocacy of Socialist Realism, in 1935; even so, his estheticism notwithstanding, Cocteau did consider art from a mere social point of view in some contributions to Aragon's own periodical *Ce Soir*, in 1937. In turn, Cocteau's comment on Rembrandt's poverty as the height of luxury is practically an allusion to Aragon's beautiful *Apology for Luxury* (1947), later included in his *Henri Matisse: A Novel* (1971). Especially toward the end, once the discussion moves into Italian painting, an inescapable convergence occurs. It is Cocteau, not the ever-radical Aragon, who recalls Delacroix's *Liberty Leading the People to the Barricades* (1830) before the *Young Standard-Bearer* of Piazzetta.

That the Dresden paintings were removed in 1945 by the Soviets and returned during the Cold War makes it difficult to establish the exact spirit in which these events took place, considering reports of those who remember the terrible days of 1945 in Germany. Once before this collection had been rescued in wartime: in 1759 paintings were sent to the fortress of Königstein during the (also virtually worldwide) Seven Years' War, when Dresden was occupied, for the second time in a generation, by Prussians. In fairness, even if Aragon were exaggerating Soviet beneficence, we would want to know more. Likewise, in the Allied bombing that razed Dresden, a city that was itself one of the treasures of German culture, 159 paintings burned (the great loss for modern art being Courbet's *Stone-Breakers* of 1849): even if this did assault the morale of Nazi Germany, can it ever finally justify what was lost to all? Suffice it to say here that, as with a human life, whoever saves a great work of art in the midst of warfare earns an ultimate gratitude.

At their humanly worst, Cocteau can seem dizzily preoccupied with ransacking art for delicious sensations while Aragon sermonizes, virtually manhandling works in the hurry of getting on to historical conditions. But at their best, Cocteau shows, better than he could have argued, that esthetic delight is beneficial to mankind, while, for his part, Aragon, the poet of the French Resistance, can evoke the inextinguishable humanity of Bertolt Brecht. Brecht himself wrote a fragmentary, postwar dialogue on painting (between 1948 and 1956), addressing its liberating value: through our very preference for one painter over another, we come to see difference as difference, instead of as opposition. If that sounds like Aragon's style of thinking more than Cocteau's style of feeling, it is nevertheless true only once one has, according to Brecht, achieved *"die nötige Empfindlichkeit für Malerei"* — the necessary sensitivity to painting.

Preliminary Discussions

As it is no great distance from the Palais-Royal to the Marché Saint-Honoré, one might as well go on foot. But there must be something unusual about this pedestrian, as people turn and stare at him, nudging each other and pointing him out. Only a sharp ear can hear them whispering: "That's the Infernal-Machine Man!" Even those who don't know who he is are shocked by his floating mane of gray hair. He has a flat in the Regency Gardens behind the Théâtre-Français, next to the window that Colette no longer looks out of; a flat not much bigger than a domino box, so that an extra double-blank would be hard to squeeze in. So people naturally wonder how he manages to assemble his famous time-bombs in there: but his skill has greatly improved since the days when, forty years ago, he planted his first heavy device in the Théâtre du Châtelet, along with two other expert artificers and terrorists, the young Picasso and the aging Erik Satie.

Today he is off to meet someone who was his enemy for many years, before the latter was partnered by a woman who changed his entire life. The two men hated one another for almost twenty years and even then, quite a lot of water had to flow under the bridge before everything changed and their enmity turned into friendship.

Our pedestrian now turns into a narrow street that survives as an odd anachronism between the Rue Saint-Honoré and the Avenue de l'Opéra. Here he salutes the memory of a famous predecessor, Dr. Guillotin, who lived at one end of the street when Saint-Just lived at the other. Before taking lodgings at a carpenter's in the Rue Saint-Honoré, Robespierre also occupied that house with its entrance in a side-street. And at number 5 (which is now a hotel), long after all their violent deaths, the carpenter's son used to pay secret visits to a certain Monsieur Teste, an even more mysterious person than Valéry's character of that name. Early in August 1830 Buonarroti, Babeuf's disciple, went into hiding at this address after his return from Brussels. But of course all this has nothing to do with our present business.

The house that our pedestrian is heading for is a fine old building that has been taken over by small tradesmen and modest wage-earners. It covers the rear and two wings of a small courtyard that was cut in two when divided between two owners. The "Infernal-Machine Man" was making for the smaller part. On the street side, a wall stretching between two carriage-entrances and painted with a muddy grain to imitate wood, includes a ground-floor shop. Above the roof of this shop sprouts an elm tree that comes into leaf every year, although its lower part has never been visible. It looked sickly enough in this summer of 1956, having been attacked by swarms of caterpillars that invaded the yard, the street, and even the caretaker's lodge.

The pedestrian now eyes this building with some uneasiness, for although he enjoys making explosive devices he is afraid of other people's. It was in this house that he first submitted his cheek to a gadget that afterwards he could never do without: an electric shaver. In those days it was occupied by a shirtmaker — not Valéry Larbaud's *Poor Shirtmaker* but a tradesman afflicted by money troubles worthy of Balzac, and who left as his monument an enormous galvanized zinc pipe that served as a dubious outlet for the workshop's gas heating and vented clouds of steam and fumes from the upper windows. Now times have changed, and it has become the Moroccan Agency, with a depot guarded by a tall, thin official who sports a turban: in the evening he removes his gaudy headgear to go shopping, reducing himself to a veteran whose three rows of medals on his chest relate the story of his life.

On the second floor the visitor is awaited by a machine that alarms him in advance, one of those contraptions from Kafka's *Castle* and with a name that could have been invented by Jules Verne: in other words, a "magnetophone." It now has to be explained that the tenant of this apartment and his neighbor from the Palais-Royal had planned to write a book together, and that neither was used to that kind of collaboration. Their pretext for the book was a complete set of photographs of the works in the Dresden Art Gallery, which had recently[1] been taken when the exhibition of the Dresden art treasures was held in East Berlin after having disappeared from sight over ten years earlier. They proposed to share them out according to their (no doubt) conflicting tastes: each would hold a pack of them in his hand and comment in his turn on whatever "card" he played. But first they had to deal them out, and to their astonishment they found that they had both made an identical choice. What could they do about it? They could no longer play a war game in which a Rembrandt takes a Pieter de Hoogh or a Velázquez clashes with a Manet. How were they to keep the ball going? When they drew the same item it would be impossible for each of them to deal with it separately and go and write about it in his own corner. Then someone suggested that they could use a tape recorder.

This is a diabolical instrument that records on tape whatever one is imprudent enough to say to it. Sometimes the tape snaps and the machine keeps on turning, producing a metallic raffle that snarls around the bobbins and cannot be unknotted; remarkably like the pedestrian's mane we have already mentioned. But the worst of all is not just such mishaps and wasted tapes, but the machine's malicious accuracy, rather like a camera's, when it does manage to catch the dialogue. Its ear will allow nothing said in its presence to pass undetected; it refuses to forgive you the slightest mannerism or waffle or sneeze. In conversation people are polite enough to catch only the gist of what the other person says, being quite used to the imprecision of speech with its repetitions, splutters, woolly syntax, and hit-or-miss expressions. When we talk we never bother about being correct: our sentences have no collar and the speaker wears no tie. We gargle with dozens of little meaningless clichés and fill up the gaps in our thinking with twaddle, adjectives in search of an idea, always busy wiping our noses in the middle of relative clauses: in short, it's an endurance test from which we are never sure of emerging with a clean sheet. Just too bad: but as there seemed to be no other way of going about it, the two accomplices decided to go ahead with their experiment.

That afternoon, at the hour when the aroma of coffee wafted from every house in the street as in a poem by Saint-Léger, the man from the Palais-Royal groped his way up the stairs in that building near the Marché Saint-Honoré, finding himself in darkness as the electric time-switch was out of order. The house was not exactly elegant: the carpet had not been relaid on the once-white stairs since the war, so that there was nothing but a sort of hollow runner tracing a path between the faded eggshell paintwork on each side. Up on the second floor, in a flat cut in half (the part on the left being occupied by a woman who made blouses), the magnetophone was lying in wait for its prey. He consoled himself that perhaps the ceiling was higher here than in his domino box; but wondered how Elsa and Louis never disappeared beneath the books in the two-and-a-half rooms they had settled in. The bell rang, then came Elsa's voice saying "No, it's not the phone, it's the door." And now it's the magnetophone's turn to do the talking.

COCTEAU: On arriving at Aragon's I see that he handles the tape recorder like an expert.

With our names on the same book, anyone might expect us to be talking about poetry — but our subject is painting.

Perhaps we should explain why the distinctions between the arts and the various genres are disappearing. The days are over when a Leonardo da Vinci asked a patron whether he wanted him to paint his wife's portrait or write a poem about her. Poetry and painting, music, sculpture, are only different vehicles for the same journey. What is your view?

ARAGON: In my view, like all art, painting is a mirror-world, a world of reflections, and perhaps it brings us two together more readily than anything else because it offers some sort of evidence of that reflection. We can understand better from a picture than from the written page what that mirror-world is. As we enter that world as into some enchanted grotto, ours is not just a superficial encounter; but all our past, all the things our lives consist of, all we have ever thought, all that has ever united or divided us, now integrates into a whole. I think this is what made us turn towards painting, towards one of those things most close to us — as indeed it is to most French people; for in France there is an uncommon passion for art, which we both share and participate in.

COCTEAU: You once mentioned that over and above all our past disagreements we are both the friends of painters. I regret our period of hostility (though not without some reservations); but this fact united us at the same time because we were both fighting for similar causes. We should now find it hard to explain our past quarrels. Well, in spite of those differences we were both interested in the same painters and, for instance, we were both friends of Picasso's, although he kept outside our conflict and somehow dominated it.

ARAGON: Or rather, he was at its very center. It was through him that we first came together, and because of him that we fell out. Why? Because our problem — what we called the Picasso Mystery — is more or less the mystery of all art and poetry. And I think that if we go into a gallery together — and since that is our pretext now, the Dresden Gallery — that mystery is what cannot be reduced to words in a man like Picasso, and it looms before us whenever we look at the reflections of all human thought, the images of Man on the walls depicting not this or that man we have known, but all their counterparts in every land and age.

COCTEAU: Yes, Picasso was the eye of our cyclone. The other day we were discussing him, at Cannes. He knows how lucky painters are. A writer produces a phantom, but a painter produces a work of flesh and blood. He is under the hypnotic spell of the immediate evidence of the senses, a language that he has to translate into another language that can be read throughout the world. He is gifted with skills that limit the scope for misunderstanding and ill humor. The toil and fatigue of work in the plastic arts cannot be compared with the solitary dramas of literature, of the art of writing. Of course there is the same difference between those who observe plastic forms and those who read a poem: but then it is obvious that you and I are untranslatable poets, while people can read a painted poem, that is to say a plastic poem, immediately — or rather, they think they can. They make the same kind of clumsy translation in their minds, but in principle it seems to serve no purpose and the canvas works on them automatically.

ARAGON: Yes, painting is an international language, and in that respect poets are at a disadvantage compared with painters, because from the very first moment when a painter faces his canvas he is no longer alone, for behind him or in the back of his mind there are those absent spectators who sooner or later are bound to become present.

COCTEAU: Unfortunately the genius or talent of painters seems so obvious, so visible, that a sort of exchange-rate soon develops round them, as is not the case with poets. Writing involves a terrible solitude. I have said elsewhere that one of the worst solitudes imaginable is a poem in the French language; even though poetry is one of the essential branches of art in France, however much the French fight shy of it. The French are sensitive to the poetic: but the "poetic" is the very opposite of poetry. It seems to me that nowadays people call anything *poetic*: a shop-window display is poetic, a woman's dress is poetic, a room or interior is poetic. The word is used and abused indiscriminately. This tragic farce is all the more dreadful as those who are so fond of the "poetic" despise poetry, whose hardness and complex simplicity alarms and baffles them.

ARAGON: But painting, on the contrary, is a confluence, a meeting point, and French painting especially so. And the French have such a passion for painting that one can't understand what it consists of. Just think of all that gets itself painted in our country. Think of the fantastic crowds flocking to our exhibitions, however small or inaccessible. There are always far more people going to look at pictures than reading poems.

COCTEAU: Inevitably, as there is so much room for misunderstanding. It is obvious that just as few people really *see* a picture as really read a poem. But they think they can see the picture because they can see what it represents. If it's an abstract, they think of it as something decorative, whereas they would be insulting the painter in praising his genius for decoration, since the abstract painter just as much as any other is expressing himself and creating his self-portrait when he paints an abstract. But most people think they are appreciating painting when they like what a painting represents, while in the case of a poem they would be required to like the poem itself; for a real poem has no fixed meaning, that is to say it is composed of extremely mysterious signs that need a sort of Champollion to decipher them. Most people read poems in the same way that hieroglyphs were interpreted before Champollion came along and discovered that they constituted an idiom. Until then people saw in them nothing but amusing or silly drawings. I dare say that in all innocence many people believe they can make contact with or "relate" to art, but they are more ready to think they can do so with painting than with poetry. They are very much mistaken.

ARAGON: That is what makes museums and galleries so extraordinary. We and our whole generation were very hard on them.

COCTEAU: I'd like to ask you something, as there are such gaps in my education. When did they start having museums and art galleries? At one time, pictures were not hung so that people could come and see them: they were used for decorating houses, mansions, and churches. They were there for the owner's pleasure, or God's. The *Burial of Count Orgaz* is hung in a dark corner in Toledo. How could it ever be seen before they had electric light? Nobody thought of hanging paintings in rows so that people could file past their corpses and identify them. Can you tell me when they started having museums and art galleries?

ARAGON: I confess that I know little or nothing about that. There were certain public collections in Greece and Rome. But I should say that art museums are a modern invention, at least in France, for I know nothing about other places. Before then only the rich and powerful could afford to buy pictures; you found them in royal palaces: when all is said and done pictures were created for kings or their financiers, but certainly not for the public to come and gape at. I suppose the museum must have come into existence with the French Revolution, after a false start earlier in the eighteenth century. Then the Directory founded some museums in the provinces. After that came the Musée Napoléon...

COCTEAU: So pictures were brought into circulation through wars and their disorders, and pillage...

ARAGON: Yes, of course, with Napoleon; then the Musée Napoléon, which was the nucleus of our present Louvre collections, was broken up in 1815 when Canova came to reclaim works of art on behalf of the allies. Later on, many works were shared out between the Louvre and the Tuileries. It was the Revolution of 1830 and particularly that of 1848 that created the public museums in France as we now know them. As you know, it was in 1848 that the Louvre collections were established on the one hand, while the Luxembourg collection was founded by Jeanron. He was a very remarkable man who is now practically forgotten. Jeanron was a painter and sculptor, a member of the Barbizon school, a friend of Daumier's, a contributor to *La Caricature*, and generally speaking a sort of utopian socialist and Christian socialist. In about 1834 he published an anonymous work called *L'Espérance*, a sort of poem in what we would call the Claudel manner on the evolution of the world, which I regard as one of the finest things in the French language. I know of only two copies of it: my own and the one in the Bibliothèque Nationale. It was never reprinted. It's quite an extraordinary book. Well, this man was the first to introduce a certain "modernisme" into painting: it was in his paintings that telegraph poles

17

and wires first appeared in 1865 or so, causing considerable scandal in the *Salon* long before Fernand Léger was born. Altogether Jeanron, now totally forgotten, played a decisive part in organizing our national collections of painting.

COCTEAU: In short, paintings were stolen after a victory and shown to the masses as trophies, rather like enemy flags. So museums and galleries were a product of imperialism.

ARAGON: Yes, but the case which brings us together today, the Dresden Art Gallery, is the very opposite, inasmuch as the war that had recently devastated the whole of Germany passed through Dresden, and it was the army of occupation, the Soviet Army, that moved the Dresden collection to Russia. As a result the paintings were out of circulation until they could be repatriated; and if we can now see the Dresden treasures in Berlin until such time as the Dresden Gallery is reconstituted, it is not because of pillage but thanks to the invader's protection.

COCTEAU: *The Wedding Feast at Cana* painted by Veronese for a room in St. George's Island is now in the Louvre. Count Cenci, who founded the admirable orphanage on the island would willingly give some other masterpiece in exchange for it. The irony is that this painting was not returned with the others, merely because it was too big for packing and transport. Count Cenci asked me to make a final appeal to the Louvre, but a negative reply was given and Georges Salles refused to return that sublime creation.

ARAGON: But in the present case it was the invader who ensured the Dresden Gallery's survival.

COCTEAU: One odd thing that is happening, especially in Italy, is that museums and galleries are turning into churches. Nowadays the tourists walk round them in silence, hardly daring to look at the works but eying one another; whereas on the contrary, even in Spain the churches are becoming museums. The tourists in churches chatter at the top of their voice with a shameless lack of decency, and stare at pictures that were never meant to be looked at: when they were donated to the churches the faithful never looked at them, but hid their faces in their hands or bent their heads to the stone floor. The mantilla that women still have to wear over their shoulders when they visit Italian or Spanish churches seems like a mockery compared to what is tolerated in other respects.

ARAGON: You bring me back to Spain, so I must mention that in 1936 I witnessed a precedent to the Dresden affair, during the Spanish civil war. With Elsa I accompanied a truck that was loaded with a film projector, a printing press for the front, and medical supplies for the wounded, for our friends Alberti, Bergamin, and other Spanish writers in Madrid. In Madrid they asked me to accompany a commission of the Republican Ministry of Education to the Duke of Alva's palace. You know what the castle is like, high above Madrid. It was then becoming a center of hostilities, being threatened by Franco's forces. I saw the Duke of Alva's art treasures being removed for safety and they asked me how to go about it, how to store them in the Madrid caves and so on. Unfortunately there were some items that could not be removed at all, such as the marvelous Gobelin tapestries which had to remain on the walls because shifting them would have reduced them to dust.

COCTEAU: As with the Mycenaean tombs. You unearth Agamemnon and he crumbles to dust — as I did in *Baron Fantoni*, a moment in the scenario that terrified Paul Eluard.

ARAGON: The young Spaniards who were guarding the Duke of Alva's gallery, or rather his home-cum-museum, were in there playing with the Duke's pet animals, looking after his canary, puppy, and kitten: those armed youngsters who were guarding all those things with no other thought than to preserve them, were in despair at being unable to save the Gobelin tapestries when the bombing began. Then the "lawful" owners began to surround Madrid. The forces and airplanes under the Duke of Alva's personal command bombarded the castle and reduced it to ashes. The Duke himself shelled and burnt his own Gobelins.

COCTEAU: Was that by chance or because he wanted nobody else to own them?

ARAGON: Because there was a war on, and because it so happened that on one side were those who were regarded as the natural defenders of art, and on the other the childish and ignorant Spanish people, denounced by the press incendiaries when they had quite rightly taken steps to defend their heritage. Such an event was not unlike the way the Red Army was denounced as a destructive force by the media although it saved and restored the Dresden collection.

COCTEAU: I have always preferred a magnificent disorder to a mediocre form of order, and I'd rather see the Spanish burning and slashing their own paintings than selling them off. They would rather destroy a work in anger than take it down, roll it up, hide it away, then sell it in New York. I like the red and yellow fire of Spain in all its forms, including the *corrida* which acts as a safety-valve for their incendiary impulses. So you have your palace defended from the Duke of Alva's fire, and the masterpieces burnt in the heat of anger.

ARAGON: That sounds very beautiful, but it is wrong. Because in fact such furious destruction never happened — whereas during our own revolution in France works of art were systematically destroyed. In Spain there is an astonishing cult of works of art, all the more surprising for us — and here I am thinking of our own generation — as all that happened in an age when artists despised museums and galleries and regarded the destruction of "art treasures" as part of the modern outlook. There was nothing like that in Spain.

COCTEAU: But they damaged the portrait of Cardinal Tavera — who looked rather like Picasso's white horse in his *War and Peace.* I saw this masterpiece at the Duchess of Lorma's, after its restoration.

Pablo Picasso
War and Peace

ARAGON: Such incidents were quite exceptional and can be traced to anarchist elements that are always numerous in Spain. But the Spanish people as a whole, on the contrary, were remarkably restrained in that respect.

COCTEAU: I should have thought of the Spanish as being quick to insult what they love. Picasso insults the human face because he loves it — isn't that the essence of Spain?

ARAGON: Agreed — but Picasso was only copying Cranach...

COCTEAU: There you are: Picasso adores idols and smashes them.

ARAGON: No doubt he has those two characteristics; but that brings us back to our theme, as for us Dresden is first and foremost the palace of Cranach, when all is said and done. Perhaps the most beautiful images we have chosen are the Cranachs, apart from some surprising works to be discussed later on. The striking affection for Cranach that was reflected in a whole phase of Picasso's work comes alive for us in this collection. Here there are many painters of widely different character. I dare say Picasso would have painted over or repainted certain canvases without the slightest hesitation — just as he does with his own, for that matter, when he tears up his canvases or paints on top of them — or just as he transforms an object into a human being or a human being into something else, or will suddenly daub great black lines across some splendid creation of his — I have no doubt that Picasso would have painted over quite a number of these artists. But he would never have painted over a Cranach. He imitated him, instead.

COCTEAU: Not long ago he joked that the real film being shown inside the cinema was Uccello's, and that Tintoretto was like one of those hacks who paint the poster on the door. Whenever Picasso is having a bit of fun or showing disrespect it is always better to go along with him. His astonishing or scandalous cracks always have some basic truth behind them. He went on to say that the less famous Italian painters were the genuine ones, and that the most famous are merely posters on the doors of art.

ARAGON: Now it seems to me that you have just defined the real subject of our discussion, as if by accident. Basically, what we are looking for in the Dresden collection is not exactly painters themselves, but those works that are *secret* pictures, and even secret pictures by great painters such as Rembrandt. The Dresden collection contains some Rembrandts, such as the portrait of the artist with his wife, that are among his most famous canvases: but for us it is just one of those posters on the door, whereas there are other Rembrandts in the same gallery that are *inside* portraits, the genuine article.

COCTEAU: To my mind we are very close to each other in this respect, although many people would think we are strangers to each other. Our closeness is proved by the fact that when we examined those hundreds of photographs of Dresden canvases, I saw that we had the same criteria. Perhaps our unanimity could be ascribed to something not unlike sexuality. Some works produce a sort of moral orgasm without which there would be nothing but platonic abstraction and dilettantism. We have both yielded to the secret charm of the same pictures, instinctively picking out what you called the *secret* paintings, exclaiming, "This is the miracle of the Dresden collection" on seeing a jar of peaches. This *Jar of Peaches* is by Claude Monet, who for us is not exactly taboo. Consequently it was worthwhile having this discussion, as we are not doing it for thrills or shocks but in order to confirm a certain kinship.

ARAGON: You have just said something that goes to the heart of our differences and resemblances. Of course I don't think or imply that you meant it otherwise than metaphorically, but I naturally want to oppose my own image to yours. Against the sexual image you apply to things I must advance my own image, which is a social one. These two things are implied in what I said at the beginning, which is that art or painting is a world of reflections. For me a masterpiece, or what makes a great painting, is something in which I most profoundly discover Man. But of course, personally, by Man I mean Man in his infinite variety, Total Man, and I would say — just as people call a poodle a caress-dog or lapdog — not merely caress-Man but Man in general, in the totality of his relationships with his fellow-men, and consequently in his complex form, which is the social form of human relationships. I think that the world of reflections into which we enter through painting is naturally the image that history cannot provide of the man of any particular period or time; because history gives us a purely linear image of such a man, whereas painting restores to us what is about to vanish forever. So you will understand that I am opposed to abstract art because it is linear, like history. You see, there is some danger of our being a generation of guilty men because nobody will paint the Gare Saint-Lazare, as for instance Monet could, with the result that nobody will know what the Gare Saint-Lazare looked like in our time.

COCTEAU: Yes, but we have photography, which didn't exist...

ARAGON: But you know full well that photography gives only a particular kind of image of things...

COCTEAU: Yes, the lens is a third eye, oddly deriving from the other two, and like painting, photography soon becomes individualized. A photographer by the name of Clergue recently brought an album of his photographs to Picasso's studio. He also sent me some others, and we were both astonished when we saw how his prints were not merely aesthetic stuff, picturesque views of the flea market or the curious shapes of flamingos frozen to death at Saintes-Maries-de-la-Mer. No, this Clergue fellow was actually *present* in all his prints. I wonder whether the role you assign to painters isn't going to be taken over by photographers, and whether in fact anything of the painter's art will survive except what remains invisible to those who are looking for no more than a duplicate, a pleonastic resemblance to the model.

ARAGON: Allow me to turn your own argument against you. When we both looked at the photographs, you felt that color photography was often more remote from the original than the black-and-white, so you thought we should have them together, side by side. Surely the same may be said of the distinction between photography and painting when they deal with the same subject?

COCTEAU: In any case something very odd has happened, Louis, which is that although the Impressionists thought they were getting away from photographic representation, we can now see that they were making splendid colored photographs.

ARAGON: Perhaps: but color photography is much less accurate...

COCTEAU: There is photography and photography, just as there is painting and painting.

ARAGON: No doubt.

COCTEAU: I am not arguing that the photographer equals the painter, but I do mean that photographic documents will show us that Gare Saint-Lazare that you want man to bear witness to in the same way as Apollinaire immortalized the Eiffel Tower or the Mirabeau Bridge.

ARAGON: Gare Saint-Lazare — no, it's not just a matter of that, which in fact gets on my nerves.

COCTEAU: Of course, I'm with you there...

ARAGON: But it's a matter of the unique beauty of our own era, the beauty of something just coming into existence. Of course I was thinking of Apollinaire, as you know: "Dread the day when the sight of a train no longer thrills you." You understand? I think that the artists who witnessed the great modern inventions conveyed an emotional image of them that nothing can replace in retrospect. Take for instance the new gas lighting in Paris — I can't quite remember that line in a poem by Charles Cros (he takes *Le Coffret de Santal* from under a pile of books) — yes, here it is: "The opera ball, the gaslit boulevards, the posters" or again, "The gas jets blaze on café terraces."

COCTEAU: And there's a similar line in Moréas, "The gaslamps lighting Paris chestnut trees." There are no longer any gaslamps and chestnut trees on the Champs-Elysées, now it's all electric light and plane trees; yet the old image survives.

ARAGON: Yes, but at the moment when things are appearing for the first time, they have a special savor that nothing can give them later on.

COCTEAU: You are quite right in clinging to the human side of art, it's the only thing that interests us, the only side that some spaceman observing us from some more advanced or differently evolved planet could not mock at. He might laugh at our science, but not at our art, whose mechanism is entirely our own and beyond his grasp. And my simple criterion is also a human one when I say that a work of art touches my soul, just as a man might say that a woman "gets under his skin." I look for nothing else, not being the kind of "intellectual" that you couldn't be either. Platonic admirations get on my nerves. You and

I coincide, you with your taste for the human and I with my transcendent sexuality; for our method of judging is direct and does not depend on academic conventions. An instinctive impulse in your case towards a fraternal humanity, and in my case towards an organism that stirs the most intimate feelings, made us both select the same works of art. What no doubt attracts you in a painting, as it does me, is that whatever the artist might be showing us — still life, landscape, or portrait — he is making a confession and always painting his own self-portrait. What attracts us, in short, is the complicity in that signal or password that a brother-man leaves us after his death. It is this signal that makes all the difference between dead works and those that go on living.

ARAGON: But the artist makes that signal primarily for himself and for his own age. For us he is not just a man in isolation, in a vacuum. And what we hear is a man transmitting things to us that without him would be dead.

COCTEAU: Yes, but pictures...

ARAGON: I mean not just the artist himself, but everything around him. Because of course he might be Uccello; but he is Uccello surrounded by men armed for battle, clad in mail and armor and all that they imply, all that could never exist in later costume. And you know what happens when one tries to perpetuate anything. Well, all right, let Paul Valéry sleep in peace in his graveyard by the sea! But for instance, in the first half of the twentieth century people went on creating in an antiquated style, and you know what sort of photographs remain of the theater or cinema of that period, full of tremendously 1900 dames. We cannot escape the fact that a man can paint nothing but the age he lives in.

COCTEAU: A collection of the productions of *Carmen* would all bear the date when the opera was staged.

ARAGON: And that is why museums are so exciting, contrary to what we said when we were young. Because the museum is the very opposite of the cemetery. It is a resurrection. But that depends of course on who passes through it.

COCTEAU: Just one point: when a painting doesn't get hung — and so many do — when it resists hanging it's because the painter somehow, in that secret code we mentioned earlier on, calls to us and murmurs "Stop! I'm not dead, here I am." His humanity attracts us more than the subject of his picture. Is that right?

ARAGON: No doubt.

COCTEAU: Good.

ARAGON: But his humanity is not just a personal humanity.

COCTEAU: Here I have to quote Goethe: "It's by hugging yourself that you are likely to reach the most people." You agreed earlier on that nobody *reads* a poet, that people just imagine they are reading poets, that we are all of us profound solitudes, and that if our work earns us a few remote friends it is because we give off some sort of phosphorescent aura. That the intensity of our life and thought creates a phosphorescence that is felt by people who would like to read us, but don't. That is why I venerate the untranslatable Pushkin. I think that in a gallery there are certain pictures that radiate that phosphorescence quite apart from whatever they represent. A human intensity, an aura, a luminous halo. Waves comparable to those that shine and radiate infinitely around a body.

ARAGON: But is it a personal aura? Is it that of the man who painted the picture or wrote the poem? Is it his alone? Or is it that of the man and his age together?

COCTEAU: Both. A union of the painter and the age in which he painted.

ARAGON: Then it's the aura of the age, all the same.

COCTEAU: This is where we rediscover one another.

ARAGON: Of course it's the *genial* atmosphere of his age, an aura transmitted through genius. But it is that of his age, nonetheless.

COCTEAU: It would never be produced, were it not for that particular man, painting...

ARAGON: Of course. Nor can it be the other way around. That is exactly where the photographer is limited by his camera's mechanism, after all.

COCTEAU: Don't you think that when people in the future look at an abstract painting, while admitting that it's very beautiful they will say "Well, this is a picture from the days when the artist thought he could get beyond forms, but had to commit suicide like de Staël because he couldn't manage it"? An artist imprisoned in forms kills himself. Even Picasso had to struggle with canvases which refused to be painted. He fought with his blood and fingernails against his prison walls.

ARAGON: Perhaps you are right. But we cannot know anything about the future, and in any case every period has its fallout. For instance, when we consider the Dresden paintings there are some that are undoubtedly masterpieces but that we pass over and leave out, just saying "of course." I don't know whether, in the end, anyone will say "of course" about abstracts. What I regret personally is that the frantic urge to abandon the epiphany of reality brings the risk that realities will pass unnoticed because the artist's contemporaries hardly noticed them, either.

COCTEAU: Yes, but you recognize like me that what is beautiful in a canvas is never just what it represents, and that the model is only a pretext for a metamorphosis. There is Van Gogh's *Zouave* and the real Zouave soldier. But even the Zouave in the watermark of *Job* paper isn't a real Zouave. The odd thing is that they have so stylized or "modernized" the Zouave in *Job* paper that a public rotten with aestheticism can recognize him at a glance.

ARAGON: One can go even further than that. If you take the portrait of a man, the portrait can be beautiful although the man is ugly. The beauty of a man is not the beauty of a painting. It is nonetheless true that in whatever is said to me there is both the man speaking and what he is saying; but in certain canvases there is only what he is saying. If the painting is photographic there is nothing except what he is saying, or if it is an abstract there is only speech without the substance of speech.

COCTEAU: Yes, but it is still a man telling something about himself in his own way. If not, it would be an empty canvas. If the abstract canvas has any interest, it is because a man is admitting himself in it, and perhaps even admitting his inability to overcome the dreary anguish of representation.

ARAGON: Now you are begging the question by supposing that the canvas has some *a priori* interest. I can't go as far as that.

COCTEAU: Careful! Then if my own criterion — I don't quite mean sexual, but of a superior sexuality — commands me, that is to say if I am suddenly attracted strongly by that painting as by a person, and if that moral "erection" I mentioned earlier is experienced, it is because the work corresponds to some organic need. It is because the canvas is an organism that exercises a charm capable of touching my own organism, if you see what I mean.

ARAGON: My reply is that, personally, I am attracted to a picture only in the degree to which it tells me something comparable to my own experience.

COCTEAU: Yes, but now you are contradicting yourself. You said before that the model may be ugly, that you can love some old concierge if she's painted by Van Gogh, or a chair, or a candlestick; but you will not be in love with that old woman, chair, or candlestick: it is true that the chair and candlestick might be Gauguin's and can move you, but not an old concierge.

ARAGON: But I am not taking my stand on the plane of love.

COCTEAU: In art there is no other plane but love.

ARAGON: I said that I don't take my stand on love because there are exquisite beauties by Boucher and others that leave me quite cold.

COCTEAU: And there are exquisite persons in real life who leave you cold.

ARAGON: That's not the point. The point is that the power and depth of art, and of painting in particular, derive from something that transcends the individual and achieves a kind of collective value that for me has nothing to do with sexuality.

COCTEAU: There must be no misunderstanding about this. When I spoke of sexuality I meant an empathy as lively, swift, evident, and strong as sexuality while having no connection with it.

ARAGON: I follow you.

COCTEAU: And not a sexual emotion, either. I want every artist to create, not as young people do nowadays, adopting their poetic or pictural stance; but to create an organism, an organic whole capable of awakening in me something like sexuality, but "dreamlike," as Mallarmé put it, "a bag of sweets, only dreamlike" as he said of his deluxe edition of *L'Après-Midi d'un Faune*. Technique seems to me — and I am not the only one, as I have heard this said by our great painter-friends and the same thesis advanced by Picasso, Braque, and Derain — technique seems to me the prime enemy of the emotive masterpiece: for the masterpiece must avoid the disaster of frigid perfection, by achieving a kind of failure. What one wants to do is never achieved and it is through the gap or fall between what one intended to do and actually does, that the masterpiece finds its grace. I believe that in the Dresden works that we chose together without any connivance, we were impressed by those that were created by that innate technique that rescues painters from inhibition, from corseting themselves and being shackled by the golden number, the golden section. The golden number being only one proof of the instinctive balance of genius, it is no paradox to say that beauty is born of failure, a supernatural false-step on the edge of the void, a fall that humanizes the shock. Thus Dali made me see that in Velázquez, if you take the hands away from the body and isolate them, you can no longer tell whether they are an old handkerchief or a scrap of paper or a bird. And suddenly those hands miraculously become hands again as soon as they are integrated into the whole. What do you say?

ARAGON: You know, that sounds like many things I heard Apollinaire say. He used to say that in Racine and other writers he could pick out phrases that contained errors of syntax, and that those errors were essentially beauties; and similarly, in prose, he said that when you have managed to write a fine period you should never stop there, but always in the end break it up by tying a sort of tin can to its tail.

German School

COCTEAU: Well, Louis, now that we have discussed our way of looking at pictures and our human way of loving painters — though we could go on for hours as we are both notoriously talkative — I think it is time we concentrated on the Dresden works, beginning of course with the German paintings.

ARAGON: Then I think, we could hardly do better than open our choice or collection with the three painters who represent the early sixteenth century: Cranach, Dürer, and Holbein, in that order so as to more or less follow a chronology of births if not of works.

COCTEAU: I find myself faced with two quite extraordinary pictures, the portraits of Henry the Pious and his lady Katharina of Mecklenburg. I don't know whether Cranach intended it or not, whether this was instinctive or deliberate, but it is more than obvious that after one's first impression a large number of details have to be interpreted in the *Henry*. He is wearing a small bonnet that is almost more feminine than Katharina's. At a more distant view the figure suggests a skeleton or some anatomical engraving of a flayed man. The pose itself is rather strange and ambiguous (I mean his way of grasping the sword) while the dog's tail is a sort of devil's appendage that appears to belong to the man.

Lucas Cranach the Elder
Portrait of Duke Henry the Pious.
Page 33

Lucas Cranach the Elder
Portrait of Duchess Katharina of
Mecklenburg. Page 33

I have just returned from Oxford, where they put a Doctor's cap on my head. I was dressed up like one of Cranach's sitters yet I remember feeling no embarrassment in the street, as I fitted perfectly into the architecture. I was robed in such a way as not to feel out of keeping with the medieval buildings I was paraded through, with an old Erasmus, the Vice-Chancellor strutting at my side. No doubt this Cranach gentleman Henry must have integrated himself in the same natural way into the life around him, but nowadays he poses a few enigmas or riddles. As I've suggested, he is a creature of myth and legend, whereas in Cranach's time he just looked like a noble among other nobles.

Now let us consider this Katharina of Mecklenburg. She looks like a little white mouse. But she also looks very sly, she is smothered in jewels and is much more feathered and plumed than her companion. There is a hint of religion or fear in the placing of her hands, as if to protect herself from the evil intentions of her diabolical husband. Incidentally, her hands recall the joined hands of the dead, and altogether her costume is more severe than Henry's obeying that law of nature by which the female is less decorative than the male. I think that in those days people conformed to the rhythms of nature more than we do now, and that is why men dressed more ostentatiously than women. Whereas he has a big hunting-dog she has only a little lapdog something like the Maltese spaniel in that painting of harlots.[2]

Now if I take away the man's little flowery hat, then his riblike doublet and that rather obscene sword, and the hose and shoes from his long narrow feet, and in short isolate him from that skeletal shell; and if I take the soft plumage from the woman's head, and remove her massive necklaces and rings, her slashed bodice and skirt, then, dear Louis, we are left with Cranach's Adam and Eve, clad in nothing but a fig-leaf, though it hardly looks like a fig-leaf to me.

ARAGON: The strange thing is that his *Adam* and *Eve*, the two figures that serve as counterparts to his Henry and Katharina and that we both selected, are quite unlike the two central figures in the great canvas portraying *The Earthly Paradise*. When we look at these products of the sixteenth century we have not to lose sight of the artist we are dealing with. Although it has not been proved, Cranach is said to have accompanied the Grand Elector of Saxony to the Holy Land. Was he portraying a vision of the Holy Land in *The Earthly Paradise* after his return to Germany? Was it his personal image of man and woman that he had in mind at the time, which was also the time of his own marriage? I have no idea. But certainly the Cranach we see here, torn between two contradictory visions — that of the natural man and woman surrounded by the creatures of paradise on earth, and the somewhat sinister specimens of the Saxon court whom you have described — this Cranach himself is a person of some consequence who played a part in that dual world. Lucas Cranach was a friend of Martin Luther and his wife Katharina of Bora: he painted several portraits of Luther and Katharina, but also of Melanchthon. He was contemporary with the Peasants' Revolt, and this has to be remembered when contrasting Duke Henry and his courtly trappings with his Adam who is a sort of peasant in all his innocence. I think that here we are facing the same problem that faced the men of the German Renaissance, who were contemporaries of Dürer and Raphael and at the same time of Giorgione and Titian, and whose social problem was not the same as ours today. We have not to forget, either, that this was the very moment when their immediate successor, Holbein, was to meet Sir Thomas More in England. It was an age of utopias. The great utopia was in all their minds, and that painting of genius is both a reflection of the new world about to dawn, and a world of dream: it is probably this dual vision that gives all this such singularity and compelling attraction for us.

But to tell the truth, even if one could undress Henry Duke of Saxony and his wife Katharina of Mecklenburg as Cranach portrayed them in 1514 only two years after their marriage (he was forty-one and she was thirty-seven) we should not find underneath the apparel of these two who were united for reasons of state, the Adam and Eve or man and woman according to Cranach. It is a theme that he frequently handled. There is the couple near the Tree of Good and Evil that used to be at

Breslau (I am not sure whether it is still at Wroclaw[3]) in which Dürer's influence can be felt in the figure of Adam, which is dated 1512. Cranach handled it again in 1528 with his Uffizi *Adam and Eve* in Florence, in which the two figures are treated like those in Dresden. And this Adam is nothing like the Henry the Pious we see him to have become in 1537 in another Dresden Gallery portrait: a bearded old man, markedly different from our 1514 "gangster," but in his mail and iron gauntlets combining his military and religious virtues — for he earned his nickname by secretly protecting Luther the Reformer, Cranach's close friend, against the other Saxon princes including his own brother George. I think we have to draw a distinction between the personalities in Cranach's portraits, who were those of the society he lived in, and his Adams and Eves who were citizens of a new world, the man and woman of his dreams faced with original sin and the moral law. Not even Katharina's and Henry's Lutheranism can make them models for the ideal man and woman: Nothing can divest them of their costumes and trappings, or their century, or their wealth: they can never be undressed.

COCTEAU: But we have not to forget either, Louis, that this couple is flaunting the wealth symbols of the Fugger Bank of Augsburg. We land into a bankers' world among feudal lords rolling in money, who from their mountain strongholds crushed the peasants in a bloody and terrifying war. Since I mentioned the outfit I had to wear as a Doctor *honoris causa* of the University of Oxford, I wonder whether such costumes originated in Holbein's visit to England? Holbein's principal portraits are of lords and ladies. Those portraits are very English indeed, and I imagined as I walked along with that strange headgear that it had something to do with Holbein's stay in England, though they assure me that all this black and scarlet came from Venice and the Council of Ten. I should be more inclined to attribute it to the meeting between Holbein and Sir Thomas More.

ARAGON: To tell the truth, it so happened that at the age of seventy-five, well into Holbein's time, he being a little younger than Dürer and Cranach, the aging Lucas Cranach became involved in a remarkable adventure. He went and followed his patron the Elector of Saxony (which one? — they were all Fredericks — it must have been Frederick the Magnificent, John Frederick the Magnificent who was taken prisoner by Charles V). Then for four years this seventy-five-year-old man was so devoted as to abandon his fortune, family, friends, and art to disappear with his master John Frederick. And it was only a year before his death that he returned in triumph with John Frederick, who had been set free. For us, no doubt the Elector of Saxony is not, as they say of novels, a positive hero in any sense, and we find it extraordinary that he should be a man to whom Cranach could link his own destiny with such devotion, while being Luther's friend and not merely his portraitist. The whole period is riddled with amazing contradictions, both religious and social. For instance, even in Flanders there were painters who became

Lutherans one day, and the next, as soon as things went wrong, reverted to Catholicism.

COCTEAU: The most flagrant contradiction was Luther himself, who forbade the representation of the human face and insulted religious images, but whose disciple was this painter Cranach who made so many portraits of him. That proves what you were saying, it is proof of the endless contradictions of that era with its extremes of luxury and poverty, destitution and wealth.

ARAGON: We also selected two other Cranachs, both very different from the ones we have seen. The first is more primitive — *The Presentation in the Temple* — and gives an impression of the old Germany. This panel of the *Saint Catherine* triptych is, on the contrary, a painting in which Italy and Germany meet and in which the backgrounds are quite like those in Sienese paintings. Isn't there also, in Leipzig, a *Reclining Nymph* by Cranach that could be reminiscent of Giorgione's *Venus Asleep*?

COCTEAU: Yes, like a girl who could figure in the dance in Botticelli's *Primavera*, with her little basket of flowers.

ARAGON: Thus Germany became the highway or bridge between Flanders and Italy, and perhaps that is what makes the German painting of that time so moving and important. It is because it lies exactly between Flemish painting, deriving from Van Eyck on the one hand, and Italian painting at its height, which had covered the distance from Cimabue to Tintoretto, that German art was a highroad for human thought: and this was no accident, as a Dürer could exchange paintings with Raphael, which is something quite remarkable as we find little in common between those two.

COCTEAU: Looking more closely at Henry the Pious, I see that, as you told me, he has the air of a mobster, a killer, and perhaps that underworld touch is emphasized by the contrast between him and the flowery cap, which he wears cocked over his left ear just as Mafia gunmen wore their fedoras in New York. Another powerful contrast is between all the luxury of his clothes and his brutal, raffish appearance with that sword being pulled from its sheath and whose hilt strikes me as ambiguous. But we were discussing more tender and naive images. You commented admirably on the Adam and Eve in the middle of the mythological garden, in which I can even see unicorns, and there's that other group in which a lamb is being held over the head of a little child who could also join the dance in *Primavera*.

And now we come to those splendid Dürer portraits. The man's toque is exactly like the velvet one that the beadles carried in front of me last week as they headed us toward the hall where titles are conferred. And the round hat we had to wear for the ceremony was exactly that toque, a wide velvet affair shaped like a tart or a pie, not the square or mortarboard that is worn with black academic dress.

Now you must tell me about Dürer's young man and that splendid

Hans Holbein gentleman holding a glove in his right hand, about to draw his sword from its sheath in some mysterious battle, and sporting what we would nowadays call a superstar beard.

ARAGON: We have selected very little Dürer, but it's striking that the man you have in your hand and whose hat you compared with the mace-bearer's in Oxford, should be a different type of young man from the character we met in Cranach.

Although they are contemporaries one would think a whole century lay between them. This one is a far more civilized character. With Dürer's technique we are entering a new epoch. We are leaving the Middle Ages far behind and witnessing the most humane aspect of the Renaissance. Is this because the sitter, young Barent von Orley,[4] is Dutch and not German? I have no idea. And when we set this other Dürer beside it, this triptych of *The Dresden Altarpiece*, we return to an entirely different manner of painting. It is frankly German with its ornate features, its flying angels and all that decorative, medieval Germanism above the three figures in the panels, the Virgin and Child in the center-piece and the two saints acting as donors in the wings. But we are far removed from the spirit of Cranach, for here we have a painter whose personality and outlook were vastly different. Dürer's man — and I am not saying this just because of his famous *Melancolia* — is absolutely the "man of sorrow."

Albrecht Dürer
The Dresden Altarpiece. Page 40

COCTEAU: The man of the "black sun."

ARAGON: Whatever were the relations or exchanges between Dürer and Cranach, Dürer being strongly influenced by Cranach, but born a year earlier and ten years ahead in his art, there is a world of difference between them. Has this something to do with Dürer's Hungarian origins? Or his travels as a young man? He is closer to the great minds of the Italian Renaissance, such as Leonardo, whose name Engels associated with Dürer's in his *Dialectics of Nature*. Like Leonardo, Dürer was also an architect, sculptor, engineer, soldier, and the creator of a system of fortifications. Like Cranach, he was a man of the Reformation and the Peasants' Revolt. But Dürer expressed his age in an entirely different way. He was not satisfied with portraits, and if Cranach depicted the Saxon princes and Reformation schoolmen in the raw, and Luther, and the Protestant middle-class, he never produced anything like Dürer's *Knight, Death and Devil* for which, according to Marx, he had Franz von Sickingen as his model, the military leader of the nobles' insurrec-tion of 1522. I call him the "man of sorrow," applying to him the name he gave to Christ. Dürer had a profound understanding of his age, from which he drew that "black light" of his.

All that marks something like the threshold of the modern world in passing from Cranach to Dürer is to be felt again when we pass from Dürer to Holbein. The modern Man who appeared with the Renaissance confirms all that was modern in Dürer's technique. Now let us look at our selection of Holbeins.

The Holbein that Jean Cocteau mentioned earlier on makes us think of the great personages at Henry VIII's court, of whom we have one here in *Charles de Solier, Sieur de Morette.* He was an unofficial ambassador of François I to the English court in 1531. A whole society tends to find its definition here, when England found its authentic portraitist in this German painter, grandson[5] of an Augsburg tailor.

The portrait of our next two personalities, Sir Thomas Godsalve and his son John, confirms the German artist's contribution to the history of English society. This contribution typifies the spread of the Reformation into Britain. The technical link with Dürer is undeniable, but the image is now more realistic and more bourgeois. John Godsalve in 1528 is not quite young enough to survive into Shakespeare's time and his idea of King Henry will not be that of the dramatic poet.

This is where painting leads us: we have covered the years from the dawn of the Renaissance into the Elizabethan age. Many aspects of that time came together in Dürer and Holbein because they were much-traveled men, passing through Italy, France, Germany, and England; while in Flanders they paused to visit a man who was a living link with the past of the Van Eycks: the aged Quentin Massys, a master whom they admired above all others.

Lucas Cranach the Elder
Portrait of Duke Henry the Pious.
1514

Lucas Cranach the Elder
*Portrait of Duchess Katharina
of Mecklenburg.* 1514

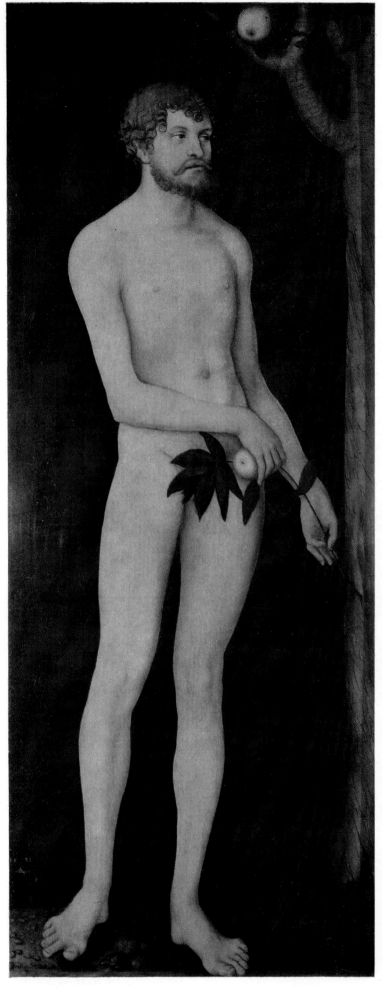

34

Lucas Cranach the Elder
Adam. 1531

Lucas Cranach the Elder
Eve. 1531

Lucas Cranach the Elder
The Earthly Paradise. 1530

Lucas Cranach the Elder
The St. Catherine Altarpiece. 1506

36

Lucas Cranach the Elder
The St. Catherine Altarpiece. 1506
Left panel: Sts. Dorothy, Agnes,
and Cunegund.

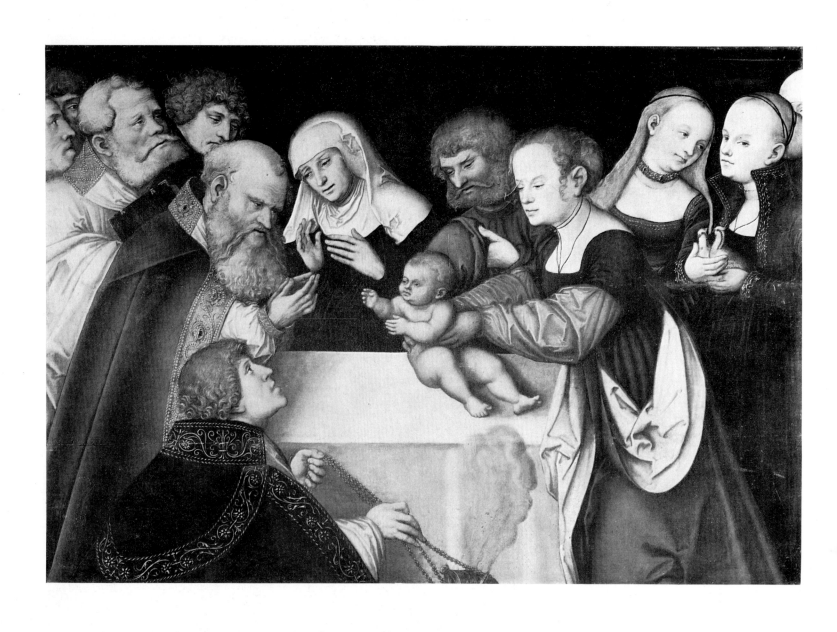

Lucas Cranach the Elder
The Presentation in the Temple.

Albrecht Dürer
Portrait of Bernhard von Reesen.
1521

38

Albrecht Dürer
The Dresden Altarpiece.
About 1496

Hans Holbein the Younger
Portrait of Charles de Solier,
Sieur de Morette. 1534/35

40

Hans Holbein the Younger
*Double Portrait of Sir Thomas
Godsalve and His Son John.* 1528

42

Flemish and Dutch Schools

ARAGON: I suggest you look at this anonymous fifteenth-century work as an introduction to the Dutch school.

COCTEAU: This Dutch *Holy Family* makes one think of certain Persian miniatures. The decorative style subdues emotion. It demonstrates once again what a miracle it was that elevated Vermeer from coldness and how, according to the painter, details can distract the eye or have a hypnotic effect.

ARAGON: That hypnosis and that lesson were something that painters kept on discovering in fifteenth-century Flanders, for instance in the Van Eycks. To confine ourselves to Jan van Eyck's marvelous *Triptych of the Virgin*, the archangel Michael watches over a kneeling donor in one panel, and Saint Catherine stands in the other, while in the center panel the Virgin is shown enthroned in a church with the infant on her knee. Everything is dominated by the architecture, with balance being given to the vertical perspective by the lance in the archangel's hand. Arches, organs, tapestries and all the riches of that time (for Van Eyck was court painter to Philip the Good[6] of Burgundy) combine for the setting to prevail over the figures. But I suggest we go straight on to consider Quentin Massys,[7] who in his old age passed the secrets of the Van Eycks on to Dürer and Holbein. Here we leave medieval immobility and static presentation behind, while church architecture gives way to the interior of the Flemish home.

COCTEAU: In *The Moneylender and His Wife*, the couple are seen swindling an honest peasant family. The woman exerts all her charm while her husband convinces the peasant that he is getting a bargain, at the same time tipping the wink to the spectator. This is a perfect genre painting, one of those themes that misled even Baudelaire as to the aesthetic value of such works.

ARAGON: Here the genre strikes me as meaningful and authentic. The peasants are offering the usurer a hen because they cannot pay the interest on their loan. The moneylender's patter, addressed as much to the observer (the painter) as to his victim, is underlined by the silver on the table, the gold waiting to be weighed, the silverware in the dresser, and the coronet on his wife's head in contrast to the peasant scarf. This canvas marks a shift away from the world of chivalry to the world of the commoner. In it we begin to witness "the icy waters of selfish calculation" as Baudelaire put it: there is no room for a Saint Michael here, where the dragon is king and will gobble the hen. But next to the aged Quentin we have one of his contemporaries,

Dutch Master, about 1500
The Holy Family in a Room with Joachim and Anna. Page 51

Jan van Eyck
Triptych of the Virgin
Center panel: The Virgin and Child Enthroned in a Church. Page 52

Jan Massys
The Moneylender and His Wife. Page 53

"the Master of the Death of the Virgin" as they call Joos van Cleve the Elder. What do you make of the remarkable contrast between these two works by the same painter, this beardless *Young Man* and the *Descent from the Cross or Deposition?* The first suggests a contemporary of Dürer, and the second all the dryness of a Bellini.

COCTEAU: Nothing could be more subtle than this descent from the cross as presented by Joos van Cleve.[8] The grimaces of pain and the model's indifference combine to produce an unreal realism, a curiously systematic but free poetic statement. Cleve's portrait of a man anticipates the portraiture of Corot, Courbet, and Delacroix — whose paintings allow nothing conventional to mask the humanity of the face. Already the painter seems to be withdrawing himself before the model and yet identifying with him, entering his body and soul to guarantee his survival.

ARAGON: To tell the truth, our choice of Flemish art would mean skipping a whole century and entering its greatest epoch, which is superbly represented in Dresden. However, we have brought in two perhaps minor but interesting painters, Hans Bol and Maerten van Valckenborch the Elder to illustrate developments.

COCTEAU: When I see the Hans Bol I admit to being quite unmoved by those tremendous drunken orgies set in Dutch landscapes. They remind me of the acute moral discomfort of the Sabbath, which I would still feel even if they stowed me underground in a deep pit.

ARAGON: And yet it was you who selected the Hans Bol landscape with Jacob's ladder and the angels! Where you see nothing but drunkards, I see the maimed peasants, brawling soldiery, murderous brigands, all the evidence of a country torn apart by war, and the perils of travel on the highroads. Bol is a miniaturist who painted with egg: only later on was he to work in oils or gouache. A painter from Mechlin, he was driven from his home town by the sackings of 1572, arriving penniless in Antwerp, and the war completely changed his way of life and his style. Now let us look at the Van Valckenborch that you selected.

COCTEAU: Painters have often been tempted by the theme of a tower that would pierce the mystery of the heavens and challenge the unknown. In a way it is the symbol of poetry trying to soar into the invisible, but unfortunately through means that make such a sacrilege ineffectual, it being on too grand a scale for both men and gods. Van Valckenborch also painted another Tower of Babel, shaped like a hive rising much higher and with a sharper point than Pieter Brueghel's.

ARAGON: You mean the one in the Kunsthistorisches Museum in Vienna? In Brueghel the tower is the essential feature; but with Van Valckenborch, who ended his life in Italy, the surrounding landscape and above all the foreground of poverty-stricken villages, and stone-cutters and laborers being inspected by a pagan king and his troops, are more significant. But the architecture of the two towers, those in Dresden and Vienna, is sufficiently alike to suggest that Van Valckenborch painted after Brueghel's manner and not just later in time. In any case neither

44

Bol nor Van Valckenborch managed to encapsulate all that the Flemish brought to painting, that multiplicity of Flemish secrets.

COCTEAU: It shouldn't be overlooked that there was such an elegance in Flanders, such a stylish elegance, that the word *flamenco* did not originate in the word *flame* as people imagine, but in *Flem* or Fleming, which means that the Spanish troops in Flanders brought back to Spain a stylishness that was unknown elsewhere. When people saw those men and their uniforms and their casual way of wearing them and striking poses, they said "there's a Flamenco!" So in Spain the term remained the equivalent of all that we mean by *chic*.

ARAGON: What I like about what Jean Cocteau has just said is the way he goes and takes the wind out of my own thesis. As we come into Flemish art we have to go back a few years, to when the country was occupied by the Spanish. We arrive or are about to arrive under the shadow of the Duke of Alva and of Egmont, and are in the middle of the period of underground resistance of the Flemings against the Spaniards. In spite of all that the Duke of Alva and his courtiers started buying up paintings, and in the process no doubt at the same time took on that dashing style that became known as *flamenco*. Scores of such paintings were sent to Spain. It is not well enough known, for instance, that canvases by Teniers were packed in the baggage of the Duke's nobles and sent to Spain, and that is how Velázquez came across them. As a result a kind of cycle was created, closing the circle between the two countries, which goes to show how painting is not just a local affair in some particular country, but a process involving society and mankind as a whole.

COCTEAU: We are back to the exchange of blood through pillage. Plunder helps the blood of art to keep in circulation.

ARAGON: But art also reveals the struggle against pillage and plunder.

COCTEAU: A cross-breeding of races goes on in our provinces, thanks to which types of great beauty emerge. There is also cross-fertilization in art.

ARAGON: In any case it is a remarkable aspect of the history of the Low Countries, as so much of their art came out of the burning and sacking of towns and so on. We see a painter living in Mechlin, setting off for Antwerp when his own place is sacked, and his whole future being changed because he happens to be in Antwerp instead of Mechlin. And in general all of the sixteenth and seventeenth centuries was torn by incredible strife. For instance, if we take one of the most famous Flemish painters, the most "official" if you like, Rubens, he was the son of an Antwerp municipal magistrate who took part in the underground struggle against the Duke of Alva, and as a result spent many years in prison. Rubens's father had traveled in Italy as a young man, but being outlawed he could only raise a family after he was set free. Rubens was born when his father was still in jail, and was only two years old when at last his father was allowed to settle in Cologne, but still under surveillance and exposed to the harsh treatment of the Prince of Nassau and his agents. So Rubens's early years were marked by extreme poverty.

COCTEAU: We have not to forget, either, that the extraordinary luxury in Flanders came from the East, from India and China, which also brought new blood into the arts.

ARAGON: But between the two Orients, the exoticisms of East and West, we find this Rubens family, unable to settle anywhere but producing this son who developed into such an exceptional character, being not only a great master in painting but also a skilled envoy, a diplomat who was summoned by Marie de Médicis but also acted as intermediary between Isabella of Spain and England, when he went there in an effort to reconcile the two enemy states that were occasionally allies. It was this Fleming, the son of an enemy of the Duke of Alva, who negotiated the treaty between England and Spain.

COCTEAU: That is very important. At that time countries had not lost their personal identity and uniqueness, and did not try, so to speak, to disintoxicate themselves. Each country cherished its own noble poisons and invented its own antidotes, each was so different from the others that painters brought something really new and unexpected with them. The tendency to iron out everything into uniformity had not yet started, they confirmed the Mosaic statement that exchanges result from imbalance. (He takes up the print of Rubens's *Bathsheba at the Bath.*)

Peter Paul Rubens
Bathsheba at the Bath. Page 59

There's not the slightest hint of the picturesque here: the costume is the flesh itself, or as Cézanne used to say, the *meat.* Nothing but eyes, nostrils, the well-curved lips, ears, curls, the splendid globes of the breasts. You sense the blood racing under the clothing. One's attention is not distracted by whether the costume is modern or not. Yet your eyes meet flesh that is dated, because the feminine type varies and Rubens's women no longer correspond to our idea of the fashionable female. Thus in Balzac the unmarriageable girl, Mlle de Grandlieu, could well be a beauty of our time, but no Lucien de Rubempré would look twice at Esther, the Rubens type.

ARAGON: With Rubens we enter into that self-contained, closed-circuit area of Flemish painting that infuriated Baudelaire. You know the frantic hatred that Baudelaire felt for such painting. And we can see what caused it. But we have to add that Baudelaire had his blind spot, because if we take Rubens's fair-haired woman we see that she has none of the provocative character of his Bathsheba: this is pure painting, we find here that stream of painting that was to triumph in Renoir and all that is inimitable in Renoir. If such Flemish sensuality means nothing to him, could he also be insensitive to Renoir's lyricism?

Peter Paul Rubens
Portrait of a Woman with
Plaited Fair Hair. Page 60

COCTEAU: Goya's *Milkmaid* is also a magnificent pre-Renoir. It is odd that the scandal of Impressionism should have occurred in France so long after the same kind of painting was accepted in Spain.

ARAGON: We don't need to go as far as Spain, a country familiar to the diplomat Rubens, in order to discover Impressionists: for instance,

Francisco de Goya
The Milkmaid

this feminine portrait by Rubens is very close to Renoir and resembles his *Madame Samary.*

Auguste Renoir
Portrait of Madame Samary

COCTEAU: You prompt me to say something important. The *Salon des Indépendants* on the eve of the war in 1913 was at the height of lyricism. There were the Fernand Léger canvases which are now in the Pavillon de Marsan in the Tuileries, and Delaunay's *Tour Eiffel*, the Douanier Rousseau's *Yadwiga*, Matisse's *Red Dancers*, Maria Blanchard's *Girl's First Communion*, Archipenko's *Gondolier*, and so on. The Aristotelian rules of Cubism came along and killed all that lyricism in the embryo. A self-appointed tribunal decided what should or should not be allowed in the harmony of the still life. We saw the reverse of the process which Baudelaire had set in motion to exalt the lyricism of Delacroix above that of Ingres, which he failed to recognize. But in 1913 the wave was strangled by the noose.

Robert Delaunay
The Red Eiffel Tower

Henri Matisse
The Dance

ARAGON: In spite of a fine quatrain about Rembrandt, Baudelaire rejected Flemish painting altogether, whereas nothing shows greater variety. For instance, we were looking not long ago at Van Eyck's triptych, so extremely dry and unemotional: but there were no more than two centuries between it and Rubens's fair-haired woman. This illustrates what you were just saying: Flemish painting rapidly covered the ground that in France stretched from the Master of Moulins or Enguerrand Charonton down to Renoir: two hundred years were enough for the Flemish eye to evolve, as against our five hundred years in France before the first signs of Impressionism.

COCTEAU: They carved elusive form, rather like Amsterdam jewelers, cutting so that beauty could more brightly shine. They cut the diamond of the beautiful into what might sometimes be taken for poisoned goblets or bloody massacres. Picasso is the same type of reckless diamond-cutter, with the radiant sharpness of his edges.

ARAGON: And all that labor, in all its forms, that went into painting, culminated at the time we were speaking of in one of its most mysterious and exceptional manifestations; the work of Rembrandt which is least reducible to a system or formula.

COCTEAU: Exactly. It so happens that black — which of course is never really black because it can only be obtained by mixing colors — favors certain works and gives them something akin to sculptural relief. It is the relief of moonlit statues that used to give some dignity to even mediocre films, whereas the colored film demands either considerable taste — which is always suspect — or unusual luck when one is being bold or taking risks.

As regards these paintings, we have sometimes set side by side colored reproductions and, let's admit it, rather neutral, grayish photographs. At one time I was disappointed by certain Gauguins, finding their coloring too flat and deliberate after having admired photographic plates of the *Three Tahitians*, which somehow seems less powerful in the original canvas. When faced with the two types of reproduction we have often hesitated considerably, for color photography is not a palette and it cannot be said that the colored photograph keeps all the painting's range of mystery, all the grace and energy the painter put into it.[9]

And yet some Impressionist canvases (and at the other end of the scale certain Cranachs), far from losing anything when you see them again in color, seem to come alive like those shells one picks up on the beach and then drops into water again. It is in order to enable the public to share our hesitations and judge of our doubts, that we have sometimes set the black-and-white and color reproductions side by side.

ARAGON: It's as if one had enjoyed two distinct mental perceptions, in black-and-white and in color, and neither gives you the picture in its entirety. In placing them alongside each other we hoped that, from the two images, the reader might construct a third image in his own mind.

COCTEAU: When they talk about their dreams, people often say that they never dream in color, or that they do. For me such a question does not arise. I do dream in color, and it plays a very important part in my dreams. But it is possible that people merely believe they don't dream in color, or else they have colored dreams but can only remember them in black-and-white. This creates a problem that rather forced us to bring the two types of print together. Spectators often tell me that my black-and-white film *Beauty and the Beast* was in color: that is how they remember it, but it was not.

ARAGON: But before coming to Rembrandt, that is to say the great painting of the seventeenth century, there is the dawn of that century to consider, and all that links it to the one before. There was a moment in Flanders when the two great painters Frans Hals and Van Dyck were the "elders," and it was only in the early years of the century, between 1600 and 1610, that the new painters such as Rembrandt, Van Ostade, Adriaen Brouwer, and David Teniers were born. Just before them were some men we hardly have time to look back on. But Van Dyck, who figures in our selection and from whom we have chosen a portrait that is equally impressive in color and in monochrome, is for us a decisive personality. This is because in our travels between the different countries, passing from Germany to Holland and returning to Italy and Spain without neglecting the relationship of those countries to England, we see Van Dyck as one of those who, like Holbein, while being a painter of Germany and Flanders played an important part in England too. Allow me to point out a curious link between him and Holbein: Holbein died during the Great Plague in London, and Van Dyck, who seemed to be following in his footsteps, is to be found traveling in Italy in his middle age. After this disciple of Rubens passed through Venice in search of the secrets of Titian and Giorgione, he was received with royal honors at Palermo before being driven out by the plague. Now this link might appear superficial; but we shall see how these men might be described as painters of the Black Death, just as we can call our own contemporaries painters of the Great Wars. We

Anthonis van Dyck
Portrait of a Young Man.
Page 61

48

tend to forget that there was a period when the plague set limits to men's lives and art, and that men staked their lives against it or had to escape. Perhaps someday this will be forgotten about times of war...

COCTEAU: I am struck by a picture that we were almost forced to select, as we have little of Van Dyck to choose from. This man is the portrait of a bird, is he not, with his winged collar and sharp robin's eye? He is pointed, sharp. His nose and beard are beaklike. He has a crested head.

ARAGON: He is an odd bird: but a bird whose influence we shall see a hundred years later in the English portraitists, who derive from Van Dyck as much as from Holbein. In the wake of this bird and of the painters who went to Italy in search of the secret of color, those Flemish painters appeared who seem to have broken completely with the Italianate tradition. We see the strange awakening of seventeenth-century Flanders in the strangeness of Adriaen Brouwer.

COCTEAU: This is a highly significant canvas by Brouwer. It conveys something of that plague that all our painters seem to have fled from. That woman standing behind the man as he wipes the child (and we know the medical role of excrements during the Great Plague), that veiled female, terrifying with her mouth gaping like a black hole, is the plague personified, and the afflicted man looks afraid of her. I think you said that Brouwer was another of those who fled the plague?

Adriaen Brouwer
Unpleasant Duties of a Father.
Page 62

ARAGON: He died of it in Antwerp. We meet the plague in London with Holbein, in Parma with Van Dyck, and with Brouwer in Antwerp.

COCTEAU: We tend to forget the man-traps in every period, all the pitfalls men had to avoid in the past; not only invasions and military occupations but diseases of every kind. Nature tries every possible way of shaking off her fleas, and men have to invent every trick to thwart her self-destructive laws.

ARAGON: So it was the right time for Brouwer's extraordinarily realistic and gloomy painting, of which this is a specimen.

COCTEAU: It goes beyond the caricatural style.

ARAGON: Yes, and it's odd to think that he was a pupil of Frans Hals. They even say that Hals dishonored himself by signing works that Brouwer had painted when he was no more than a youth of nineteen.

COCTEAU: You said this painting has an amusing title?

ARAGON: Yes: *Unpleasant Duties of a Father.*

COCTEAU: The father is wiping the little boy's behind, while in the background stands a woman who no doubt symbolizes the plague. That woman isn't just a "pest" in his house, but the Black Death itself.

ARAGON: And Brouwer himself died of it at the age of thirty-two.

COCTEAU: What a face she has — draped in a veil of spiders' webs. She's a phantom, a ghost. A red ghost, if I remember rightly. She is horrible, she stinks.

ARAGON: The two other painters we chose from that period were five years younger than Brouwer. They were born in 1610, and Rembrandt was born just between Brouwer and these two, but was to outlast and outshine them. What we find here is more typically Flemish: isn't Van Ostade the very image we have of Flanders?

COCTEAU: We are back to tosspots and codpieces.

ARAGON: Like Brouwer, Van Ostade was also a pupil of Hals and as far from Hals as can be imagined, in fact a painter of Haarlem.

COCTEAU: Drinkers and pissers.

ARAGON: Here's a scene in a peasant interior...

COCTEAU: Drunken cronies.

ARAGON: Early in his career Van Ostade imitated Brouwer, but strangely enough ended by imitating Rembrandt.

COCTEAU: The picture has a remarkable structure of lights and shadows.

ARAGON: Which anticipates the future. But from that same period we have this canvas we selected, this woman...

COCTEAU: Who looks rather Spanish...

ARAGON: I don't know about that, though there is something Spanish about her. This was by Frans Hals's son, Jan Hals, who died rather young, in about 1640. The painters of that generation were short-lived except for Teniers the Younger, who survived until the end of the century, dying in 1694.

COCTEAU: Perhaps his prudence helped: he was less subtle, less cunning, and less vulnerable than the others.

ARAGON: We selected two entirely different pieces by Teniers. The first is this seascape called *Fishermen on the Dunes*, which represents one aspect of scenic painting at that time.

COCTEAU: As dull as a visit to the Salon of French artists when we were children. The painter Gérome kept the President of the Republic out of the Renoir room, saying "Don't go in there Mr. President, it's a disgrace to France!"

ARAGON: Anyway, it's still far from what landscape was to become with Hobbema. The second by Teniers is a popular type of scene that we chose because it illustrates a quite different aspect of this painter: *Peasants Playing at Dice*.[10]

COCTEAU: Yes, you showed me it earlier on: much less alive than the others.

ARAGON: After beating about the bush, we now come to the point with Rembrandt, four years younger than Teniers, only a year less than Brouwer. With Rembrandt we reach a major crisis in art that requires a proper perspective.

COCTEAU: Every gallery has a few mischievous paintings that are killers that murder other pictures. The culprit is almost always a Rembrandt, ambushed in a dark corner. It's hard to hang anything near the great English Rembrandts. One sometimes wonders whether all other painters haven't been tempted to climb higher than he did and, finding it impossible, tried to smash the rungs of his angel's ladder.

One wonders whether he wasn't the greatest outsider in the whole

Dutch Master, about 1500
*The Holy Family in a Room with
Joachim and Anna.*

Jan van Eyck
Triptych of the Virgin. 1437
Center panel: The Virgin and
Child Enthroned in a Church.

Jan Massys
The Moneylender and His Wife.
1539

Joos van Cleve
Portrait of a Beardless Man.
About 1520

Joos van Cleve (?)
Descent from the Cross. (German
Master, sixteenth century)

Hans Bol
Village Festival in Front of the
Church and Castle. 1582

56

Hans Bol
Jacob's Ladder.

Maerten van Valckenborch
The Tower of Babel. 1595

Peter Paul Rubens
Bathsheba at the Bath. About 1635

58

Peter Paul Rubens
*Portrait of a Woman with Plaited
Fair Hair.*

Adriaen Brouwer
Unpleasant Duties of a Father.

Adriaen van Ostade
Peasants Carousing in an Inn.

63

Jan Hals
Portrait of Frau Schmale. 1644

David Teniers the Younger
Fishermen on the Dunes.

David Teniers the Younger
Chalking the Score in the Alehouse.

Rembrandt
The Falconer (Self-Portrait). 1639

Rembrandt
*Portrait of Saskia van Uijlenburgh
as a Young Girl.* 1633

Rembrandt
Saskia with a Red Flower. 1641

Page 70:
Rembrandt
Ganymede in the Eagle's Talons.
1635

Page 71:
Jan Vermeer van Delft
Girl Reading a Letter. About 1657

Jan Vermeer van Delft
Matchmaking. 1656

Meindert Hobbema
The Water-Mill.

Jacob Isaacksz van Ruisdael
*The Jewish Cemetery near Ouder-
kerk.* After 1670

74

history of painting. What do you think? Isn't it a fact that with Rembrandt we are on a peak, perhaps the highest peak of painting, face to face with the exemplar and archetype of the innate technique I mentioned yesterday? And the more we study his canvases, the more we see that not one is like another, that he struck a sort of chord once and for all, but with every note remaining distinct although the chord was authentic and had nothing fanciful about it. In talking about Rembrandt I feel that we are practically forced to speak of him as a poet, for his technique is so natural, so native to him that it seems childish to say that his pictures were painted with "genius." His technique transcends all techniques. He is one of those androgynous supermen described by Nietzsche. Now here we have two pictures, one showing a man holding a fowl...

ARAGON: A bittern or kestrel.

COCTEAU: We have this man with plumes in his cap and waving a bunch of feathers; or this mischievous woman with her saucy hat and a redhead's beady eyes; or this other woman with her hand on her breast, the same model in a different pose; and this grotesque Ganymede, an outsize baby being carried off by an eagle that looks like an old monocled rake. And look at the huge shadowy hand of the child who had been gathering cherries and is trying to push the eagle away. He had been eating cherries but the eagle wraps around him like a stage curtain with a gold tassel; you can see his behind and the infantile sex, the whole composition soars upwards with that unreal realism that creates a surrealist atmosphere, something like a collage by Max Ernst.

Rembrandt reminds me of the range and amplitude of Chaliapin's voice. One day during a rehearsal of *Kovantchina* in the Monte Carlo theater, I was sitting next to Chaliapin. Without the least effort, he was humming through his own part. When I asked whether he would be singing that evening he replied that he never *sang*, but always hummed or went through his part in an undertone, *sotto voce,* so as to leave himself a good margin. I am reminded of that "margin" whenever I see a work by Rembrandt; for although he gives out more than anyone else, he always keeps something in reserve. He rations his breath, and that is how without the least fatigue he achieves that sublime throwaway effect without which you have to show your cards or denounce your skill and technique. In Rembrandt the mystery of painting, of figurative art, is total and absolute. With all his wealth he contrives to look poor. His poverty is the height of luxury, like the luxury of those anarchist students in Salamanca who wear rags and gold necklaces at the same time. Faced with Rembrandt's works we could quote Picasso: when he was asked why he never went to America, where they would build him "a golden bridge," he replied "And I'd sleep underneath it." Rembrandt is a princely hobo bedding down under a golden bridge, but never begging as he is rich enough to start with.

To sum up, there is a language of art that resembles no other form of speech, and this savage, aboriginal, yet immensely refined tongue, in

Rembrandt
The Falconer (Self-Portrait).
Page 67

Rembrandt
Portrait of Saskia van Uijlenburgh
as a Young Girl. Page 68

Rembrandt
Saskia with a Red Flower.
Page 69

Rembrandt
Ganymede in the Eagle's Talons.
Page 70

its way both primitive and decadent, a mixture of dawn and dusk is, strange though it may seem, a universal medium like a tom-tom through which we can all communicate with each other. Across the ages, transcending the centuries, countries and nations, parties and schools and races, we aristocratic anarchists, kings to end kings, communicate through art.

At about half-past one two days ago I went into number 10 rue d'Anjou, where I lived with my mother in our "heroic" days. As I passed through the tall carriage doorway a glance towards the porter's lodge made me think "I'm late for lunch, my mother will be vexed." As we look at these slides I feel myself back in school in the rue La Bruyère, back in my childhood with the magic lantern and the green box full of slides. Our reunion occasioned by these discussions of the Dresden Gallery thus becomes a bouquet of my boyhood memories, and of those seventeen "terrible years" as Eluard called them, when those private quarrels that now seem incomprehensible made us lose the delight of communing together in front of these epiphanies. We washed our dirty linen in public instead of setting up the screen and projecting our dreams on it.

ARAGON: Now that you are emerging from the *chiaroscuro* of Rembrandt, we come to Vermeer, the most wonderful and genuine "magic lantern" of all.

COCTEAU: Yes. It can be said that every beautiful work in painting is abstract. Figurative realism is only a mask over the internal expression or *inscape* of the picture. In the same way certain superior minds mingle among us, disguised as physical bodies. Vermeer is the prince of such arcane beauty. He was hardly noticed in his own time, though people certainly saw Pieter de Hoogh. No doubt Vermeer's supreme elegance made him invisible, because unfortunately it has to be admitted that one can only contact the vulgar through some secret vulgarity. Today what I would call Vermeer's astrological logic has become visible to us, his sublime uniqueness now triumphs over Pieter de Hoogh's middle-class caution. But it is quite probable that he still isn't really seen by those who imagine they see him, and that most of his admirers are only admiring the innocent gaze of his girl in a blue bonnet, her pearly complexion, the painter's black-striped overall as he turns his back on his model, or the creamy milk pouring from the milkmaid's jug. But the abstract pattern underlying all those pretexts for the subtle organization of volumes and colors remains, I dare say, just as invisible or unseen as at the time when it was painted, when Vermeer carried his painting to a Delft[11] baker in exchange for a loaf of bread.

ARAGON: Vermeer was a poor man who was never to enjoy the destiny of such predecessors as Frans Hals, Van Dyck, and Rembrandt. Even long after his death nobody wanted his canvases. It was an Englishman, Reynolds, who first did him justice. But Reynolds did not manage to create a fashion for Vermeer. That had to wait until the 1840s when Thoré-Bürger (who also discovered Courbet) set Vermeer above all

Jan Vermeer van Delft
Girl with a Turban

Jan Vermeer van Delft
Allegory of the Artist

other painters and gave him the status he enjoys now. We have chosen two of his works from the Dresden collection: *Girl Reading a Letter* on the one hand, which is a Vermeer classic, and another which cannot be compared with anything else, with its strong figures in the foreground taking up the entire space, and which is modestly entitled *Young Girl with Her Bridegroom* on the back of our slide. This is an odd title: she is undoubtedly a girl with a young man beside her, but the picture is out of the ordinary because it has so little of the Vermeer atmosphere and is characterized by a striking lack of intimacy, unusual in this artist who is the most intimate of painters. Perhaps this may be explained by the fact that this picture is commonly known as *Matchmaking* or *The Procuress*, and that was surely Vermeer's own title for it. This was the first canvas signed by Vermeer, and dated 1656. It is his third known canvas, a youthful production — though in fact the other painting we chose and which I called a classic Vermeer is dated only a year later, 1657.

Jan Vermeer van Delft
Girl Reading a Letter. Page 71

Jan Vermeer van Delft
Matchmaking. Page 72

COCTEAU: What strikes me also is the supreme misunderstanding in all that. Because when you look at this astonishing Vermeer painting, which neither of us knew before, you feel as if you were looking at some picture-postcard sent from another world by someone who died long ago, or by some somnambulist in a world of waking men. There is something unbelievable about it. I must repeat that such realism is totally abstract, and the distances between the people and the objects, between one person and another, between the furnishings and the figures, are something astronomical. One has an impression of the illusory stillness of the heavens, a sky furnished with immovable stars.

ARAGON: With Vermeer we enter a world of "damned" painters rather than "damned" poets. Here this artist, so completely a painter of the cosy bourgeois interior and whose secret of beauty now looks so obvious, and who was neglected for two hundred years whereas the works of his Flemish contemporaries enjoyed a vogue that was denied him — this artist who died at the age of forty-three leads us directly to Meindert Hobbema, six years his junior, who lived to be seventy or seventy-one — and who I think does not particularly please you.

COCTEAU: No, but I should like to add an aside here, as you have touched on something very serious. Of course I mentioned a misunderstanding, and then you suddenly mentioned "damned" painters, almost "damned" poets in connection with Vermeer. Here we are in the presence of our modern drama: which is that since and even before Van Gogh people have grown accustomed to monsters. The monster is king. Of course a young man coming along today with the same qualities as Vermeer, though different, would pass unnoticed because people are so used to monsters that they would take him for a mere charmer, a sort of crooner. We wouldn't recognize him in our time, any more than they recognized Vermeer in his. Surrealist? No. Naive? No. Abstract? No. Therefore nothing at all.

ARAGON: It is precisely that ignorance of beauty in depth that confronted Vermeer, that we also find affecting Hobbema: the same phenomenon because Hobbema, also, died in poverty and nobody took him seriously for a century and a half. And Hobbema was disadvantaged in quite another way...

COCTEAU: Actually, Hobbema's name rather comically reminds me of Louise Abbéma, a painter commonly regarded as not worth mentioning. Well, I have seen her portrait of Sarah Bernhardt, which they say was touched up by Manet. This is quite possible. With the passage of time the portrait has taken on a certain relief, a certain charm, and indeed I shouldn't mind having that lovely thing on my own wall.

ARAGON: Hobbema's case is far more serious. Because if the charm of Vermeer's interiors seemed too obvious to be repeated after Brueghel and Rembrandt, with Hobbema it was something else — the landscape itself, that was condemned: for he began painting landscapes before anyone else.

COCTEAU: Human relationships in those days had a liveliness which overshadowed the surroundings in which people went about their business. Interiors counted less than conversation, and exteriors less than what was going on in them.

ARAGON: Yes, or they were only regarded as accessories. The landscape was not enough for Hobbema's contemporaries, so something had to be added on. In any case the painters of Hobbema's time, or at least those of any importance, were well aware that he was a great artist. The best proof is that many of them painted human figures into his landscapes.

COCTEAU: As others did in the case of Claude.

ARAGON: The figures added to landscapes were executed by specialists, and what they called *postiches* or fake additions were widespread at that time: but the fact is that a landscape painter like Claude Lorrain had his figures inserted by experts who were always less distinguished than himself. But the very opposite happened to Hobbema. His famous colleagues did him justice in doing a secondary job for him. In Hobbema there are some features that we don't meet again before Postimpressionism. Our present canvas — some sort of mill — is not enough to prove my point, but I remember a Hobbema in the National Gallery in London, dated 1689, *The Avenue at Middleharnis,* that shows nothing but a highway lined with trees.

COCTEAU: It is almost a modern highroad as seen by Courbet. There are some highly theatrical settings by Courbet in which the actors are rocks and trees...

ARAGON: You know what it reminds me of? The landscape seen through the windscreen in Matisse's *My First Trip by Car* — and in a sense Hobbema was our first trip by car.

COCTEAU: That was when Matisse could have achieved greatness, but as Picasso said, he was afraid of his own shadow. He was on the verge

Meindert Hobbema
The Water-Mill. Page 73

Meindert Hobbema
The Avenue at Middelharnis

of something very important in the canvas you mention, also in that one of a child by an open window that is in the Museum of Modern Art in New York.[12] You felt that something enormous was about to happen. But he took fright. The bourgeois in him defeated the anarchist. The *fauve* or wild painter turned into a pussycat. It's a great pity. For the rest it seems to me that in his recent works Picasso himself is squandering his rich inheritance. But show me a Hobbema, let us look at it together. Perhaps I can get over my distaste for the subject, my dislike of painters who go out hunting in the morning, to kill a view and bring it home in their bag.

ARAGON: This is the Hobbema we chose: have a look at it.

COCTEAU: It looks like a murder site in a detective novel, such as I'm addicted to. More genius is wasted in minor literature than anywhere else. There's some deadly plot going on in that mill, don't you think?

ARAGON: It's only a water-mill.

COCTEAU: A sinister mill. I'd like to see it in color, oozing blood.

ARAGON: Unfortunately we haven't got it in color.

COCTEAU: That's a pity — perhaps it would look less off-putting.

ARAGON: For me there is something in Hobbema that is not to be found in any other Flemish landscape painter. One of the dramatic aspects of history is how it enables us to explain things about other people. On the other hand I've never been able to explain my own self.

COCTEAU: That is why you chose this canvas. As soon as one explains the beautiful, it collapses. After the sphinx Vermeer we now have to salute the sphinx landscape...

ARAGON: This particular sphinx was buried in the sands for a long time. Like Vermeer, Hobbema had to wait for Bürger-Thoré. Hobbema is a modern invention. There's a strange picture by him, *The Country House,* in an American collection, that you could take for a Douanier Rousseau. And some details in Hobbema anticipate Seurat.

COCTEAU: Isn't that because some statement has been well put? Because when a statement is neatly expressed, people tend to read it with only half an eye, without pausing. It seems to me that people are only interested and brought to a halt by flourishes; but the grand style is something very difficult yet very simply stated. Isn't that what strikes us in our favorite poets, and in Vermeer and Hobbema? Hasn't this canvas we are arguing about, that extreme simplicity? I was wrong in saying it has the "tragic" atmosphere of the detective novel, as the more I look at it the less I feel that. Now it seems to me very human: no doubt one could live in such a landscape.

ARAGON: But apart from what we read into Hobbema's work, or what really is in it, it has a certain gift of light, though it's odd that I should stress this in a reproduction of a picture in which shade dominates, as in this one: what I mean is that his light is a modern light. I think the tragedy of Hobbema is that he was not understood because his light was that of our time and not his own.

COCTEAU: We have been pestered with landscapes of this sort, which inevitably date. What saves a painter is what is timeless in his style. Nothing dates this painting; neither the theme, the pretext, nor the way it is handled: but frankly, if this painting were a window, so to speak, it is one that I would not open.

ARAGON: Nonetheless here is a man who identifies with his own country, an artist with a profound feeling for his own land. He is not outside time or place, but Flemish, and here he is showing his own homeland. Even as I say that, I remember the fashionable theory about Hobbema: has it not been asserted that his landscapes were *imaginary*? Or to be more precise, that his landscapes were not copied from nature, but from existing paintings, a montage of features that he copied and reassembled. They go so far as to say that most of his little world was taken from a picture by Ruisdael, *The Jewish Cemetery,* which incidentally is in the Dresden collection. It has been claimed that he rearranged the details of the cemetery without adding anything but the figures. Georges Brouilhet, the most important critic of Hobbema, made a fine remark about this: "Hobbema's countryside is a paradise of light and serenity: it emerged from the black shadows of a cemetery in which there shines a rainbow of graves and flowers, all draped in the magnificent mantle of foliage provided by Ruisdael's oaks."

However disturbing Brouilhet's formulation of this theory might be, we cannot accept the idea of a rehandling of Ruisdael's cemetery without certain reservations. It is not enough for Brouilhet to assert that "graves become mills, rivers become ponds, the sky is progressively changed like a series of stills in a film, the same trees stand and grow in picture after picture." No: as soon as tombstones turn into mills, they are no longer tombstones. None of this explains how what we might call Hobbema-land, the great country created in his canvases, amounts to a portrayal of the natural scene a hundred and fifty years before the Barbizon school, and how he discovered precisely what the pioneers of open-air nature painting were to find, as well as Millet and the Impressionists and Postimpressionism (which Brouilhet confuses with Futurism). If all this came out of *The Jewish Cemetery*, what a cabbalistic bit of black magic it must have been! But however much Flanders has been devastated by constant warfare since Hobbema's day, now in the twentieth century we can still see that countryside as he was able to see it with all the accuracy of foresight: a vision that remains valid even though the trees he painted have all been felled, the mills burnt down, the horses slaughtered, and the folk forgotten.

COCTEAU: He achieves the exactness of poetry. All those men are ciphers, numbers, exactly the opposite of what we imagine poets to be, what we imagine that terrible poetic atmosphere to be in which the world bubbles and boils. Hobbema was liberating his inner genius in the truthful image of that house, those trees.

Jacob Isaacksz. van Ruisdael
The Jewish Cemetery near
Ouderkerk. Page 74

English School

ARAGON: Imagine that we suddenly come face-to-face with the man who loved Vermeer and Hobbema a hundred years before Thoré-Bürger did: I mean Reynolds. We have very few English works from Dresden and have chosen Reynolds who, of course, takes us beyond Hobbema's time, for with Hobbema we are barely entering the eighteenth century, as he died in 1709 but gave up painting in about 1690. English painting began in the eighteenth century. Before that, Holbein and Van Dyck went to Britain and the English were satisfied with what came their way, until Reynolds suddenly appeared. He is perhaps not their greatest but is the first of the English school, and threw a sharp retrospective light on earlier painting, especially Flemish. Reynolds lived from 1723 to 1792. He discovered Vermeer, founded the Royal Academy of Art, and became the greatest portraitist of his age. He absorbed the lesson given by Van Dyck a hundred years earlier and applied and interpreted it. He was also a forerunner of the first artists after Hobbema to paint landscapes in the modern sense of the term, for modern landscape was born in England in the late eighteenth century, before the French took it up. The great English triumph in art was the landscape, and the taste for it came from Flanders.

From the eighteenth century onwards most of the Hobbemas came into English collections, but between him and the modern landscape painters stands Sir Joshua Reynolds. The portrait of his that we are now viewing is the rather oddly titled *Mr. William James in the Costume of the Dunstable Hunt.*

Sir Joshua Reynolds Portrait of Mr. William James in the Costume of the Dunstable Hunt. Page 87

COCTEAU: This Mr. William James, as you call him, could be looking straight at a Vermeer. There is no mockery in his smile. He looks surprised at something, but makes no effort to defend himself with that beautiful left hand, which is marvelously lit.

ARAGON: When Reynolds died we were already into modern times, as the French Revolution had begun. We shall leave Reynolds in his grave in St. Paul's cathedral — though I think the church was bombed and am not sure if his tomb is still there.

COCTEAU: This gentleman, Mr. James, could well belong to that set who met the future Lady Hamilton on the river. They used to bring hampers and paintboxes with them. They dined, painted, then seduced a young peasant girl who became a fashionable beauty.

ARAGON: I don't know who he is, but in him I see mainly that transposition of Van Dyck's essential message to the English, from which they drew their painting. A lesson learnt a century later.

Now I think we must make a sort of loop in time, and having reached the eighteenth century via Flemish painting, to the threshold of English painting, we must return to another source of the modern style, that is to say Spanish painting, which is another head of that hydra we saw grappling with history in Flanders.

Spanish School

COCTEAU: What is fascinating about Spanish painting is that the struggles of French Impressionism never had to be suffered by the Spanish painters, although without the Spanish, French Impressionism could never have existed. Now we can look at some of their works.

ARAGON: When we come to Spanish painting, the strange thing is that it is summed up in a man called El Greco, from Crete, who learnt his art in Italy. This paradox was typical of their painting, so that we — I mean this for you and me in particular, for whom Barrès was so important — naturally had to turn to El Greco first.

COCTEAU: And he was long neglected in Spain itself. Do you know that Zuloaga bought Grecos for a song when the slightest thing by Goya was worth its weight in gold?

ARAGON: It's astonishing how the Spanish tend to forget where El Greco started from. He was the son of a Cretan glassmaker, and came to Venice not as a painter but along with other jewelers and glassmakers: that is where El Greco's art began in the craft of jewelry which is poles apart from his painting.

COCTEAU: Gongora called him "that odd alien from Toledo."

ARAGON: After Venice, he went over to Rome and began painting there. There were only two known canvases of his before this one we found in Dresden: a portrait of his friend Giulio Clovio, a young painter who introduced him into Roman society; and a youth blowing on an ember. Then came this third picture which he signed (as before) *Domenikos Theotocopoulos*. It is so unlike a Greco that for many years it was taken for a Veronese. It is called *Christ Healing the Blind Man.* This youthful work is in a sense earlier than Spanish painting. It was from this blind man opening his eyes (to painting) that El Greco started off, crossing the sea to Toledo where he was to live and paint for so long. He was a pupil of Titian's as well as being influenced by Tintoretto, Palma Vecchio, and Bassano. With the present work we are still far from Spanish painting in the real sense of the term. It contains, rather, the essence of Italy brought across the seas by a Cretan artist. With fifty years between them were two men of destiny in Spain neither of whom was Spanish: one invented painting and the other invented America.

COCTEAU: Now I'm looking at the picture, the only one we have here by El Greco. In *Christ Healing the Blind Man* — with a Veronese dog sniffing in the foreground — under those draperies on the right you can already see the healthy calves and ankles that show under the

El Greco
Portrait of Giulio Clovio

El Greco
Youth Blowing on Charcoal

El Greco
Christ Healing the Blind Man.
Page 88

priest's cassock in *The Burial of Count Orgaz* and later in Cézanne's bathers. It is as though, thanks to some magic trick with time — for I doubt whether Cézanne imitated the cassock pattern — El Greco had stuck a bit of Cézanne onto his own canvas. Those stout calves and fine ankles, such as one sees in deforming mirrors, reappeared later on in Salvador Dali, the prodigal son from Barcelona.

ARAGON: It is a striking fact that whereas we saw painters from Flanders and Germany going to Venice in search of the secret of color, on the contrary this man went to the same country and among the same painters in search of the secret of *blackness* in Tintoretto, Titian, and Palma Vecchio. So while the lesson of Venice spread through the medium of color in the northern countries, on the Iberian peninsula it threw a great shadow called El Greco.

COCTEAU: We also know that El Greco never left his studio, and lengthened the shadows of his models on the walls by the use of candles. He was like Picasso in the sense that he never knew if it was raining or the sun was shining outside. He lived with his curtains drawn. He lived in the shade in the mad sunshine of Toledo. He was a nocturnal painter, as you said. And look — in this painting you can already see the rifts in the sky through which the angels will come whirling down with their toes touching the tips of standards.

ARAGON: Through El Greco we come to the really Spanish painters, who were his juniors by thirty or forty years. First there was Ribera, nicknamed *Lo Spagnoletto* or the "little Spaniard." Just as El Greco who wasn't Spanish came and settled in Toledo, so Ribera left Spain and settled in Naples. But it would be hard to imagine anything more Spanish than the picture you are now looking at, his *Saint Agnes with the Angel.* The curious thing about Ribera is how he learnt his painting in Spain and brought it to Italy, though not without a spell in Venice where he tried imitating Caravaggio, in which he was not successful but merely filled his work with charm.

COCTEAU: Who is this saint?

ARAGON: Saint Agnes.

COCTEAU: She looks as though she is being draped by the angel although he is pulling the cloth away — one of those typical El Greco cloths, all stiff and brittle like something hung out to dry and thrown over a mandrake.

ARAGON: Yes, that angel in the air is tugging the drapery in such a way that you can't tell whether he is dressing or undressing her.

COCTEAU: He is undressing her.

ARAGON: No, I think that in fact she was stripped at her place of martyrdom, but God sent her this sheet to protect her modesty — a miracle completed by the hair, which suddenly grew very long so as to cover her. The little angel holding one end of the cloth has a frightening resemblance to the angels and demons in Goya's skies, and which we also meet in the *Verve* Picassos.

COCTEAU: Exactly. This angel is quite unlike those in El Greco's *Apocalypse,* with their dilated nostrils. He is charming and related to the clownish *putti* in the caricatural series in *Verve.* The upper part of the Agnes figure is beautiful, but the leg has a leprous appearance.

ARAGON: It seems that Ribera at first gave his Agnes the face of his own daughter, who was seduced by a Neapolitan noble. Then he had to replace it with an anonymous face at the request of the nuns in the convent where it was to hang. Here we sense a painter who wanted to create paintings with charm, but gave it up for lack of success to become a court painter to the Viceroy of Naples, who was a Spaniard and wanted the harshness of Spanish art. As a favorite of the Viceroy, the Duke of Alcalà, was Ribera hoping to be the only painter in Naples? They say that he was a ruthless man who drove out or ruined any painter who came on the scene.

COCTEAU: There is something harsh about this painting. It reminds me of Machado's "Castille, robed in rags, despising all you do not know."

ARAGON: And yet there was one painter he did not drive away, a painter who came to Naples and became a friend of Ribera's, and who persuaded Philip IV to buy some of Ribera's works back in Spain, just as Ribera had persuaded the Duke of Alcalà to acquire some by Velázquez. The painter in question was of course Velázquez himself.

COCTEAU: With Velázquez we are now coming to something of great importance.

ARAGON: We have two of his works here, and probably a third somewhere. Two male portraits, one called *Portrait of an Old Gentleman in Black* and the other a *Portrait of Gaspar de Guzmán,* an innocent enough image when one considers the sitter's striking and rather forbidding face.

Diego Velázquez
Portrait of a Gentleman. Page 92

Diego Velázquez
Portrait of Gaspar de Guzmán.
Page 90

COCTEAU: Rather a terrifying, dwarf's face?

ARAGON: Yes — but do you know who Gaspar de Guzmán was?

COCTEAU: No.

ARAGON: He was the Count of Olivares, Minister to Philip IV.

COCTEAU: A devil! His coat of arms showed a well with the inscription "The more you take the more I make." That was his family motto.

ARAGON: Yes, he was Richelieu's ill-fated opponent.

COCTEAU: The hand is very carefully painted, though as I mentioned earlier, Dali once remarked that he often painted hands in such a way that if you removed them from the body they would look like a child's handkerchief or a shapeless rag — as in the other portrait by Velázquez that we have here, the Juan Mateos.[13] There is genius in that indifference to detail, the sublime carelessness in these hands. The portrait reeks of hard riding and bootleather.

Diego Velázquez
Portrait of Gaspar de Guzmán.
Detail of Hand. Page 91

ARAGON: Velázquez could be called the Cervantes of painting.

COCTEAU: The more we look at Velázquez and the more we read Cervantes, the more astonishing they become. Nobody could be wiser or madder than they.

ARAGON: You know, Velázquez's fine "Lances" picture which is in the Prado has some connection with an extraordinary incident during what I think was his first voyage to Italy. (I have to add that it was not his own idea to go to Italy, but he had been corresponding with Rubens. When Rubens came to Seville to see Velázquez he convinced him that no painter could afford not to see Italy: so it was that Rubens, coming from Flanders, sent Velázquez off to Naples.) Well, when Velázquez embarked he found himself with Ambrosio Spinola, the victor of Breda. That was in 1629, but it was eighteen years later before he painted his *Surrender of Breda* in 1647: this was the famous "Lances" picture, a memento of his conversations during that dreary voyage — as it was in those days — from Seville to Naples.

COCTEAU: It seems surprising that we have no female portraits by Velázquez, none of those horrid puppets with pink ribbons. He painted women whose faces were already painted in a different sense. That is why his men interest me, showing themselves without makeup or masks, or at least nothing more than their natural masks of beards and wrinkles.

ARAGON: What about this Guzmán here, this Olivares who made Velázquez Grand Marshal to the court? The upshot was that Velázquez was sent to the Isle of Pheasants on the Bidassoa where the marriage ceremony of Maria Theresa and Louis XIV was celebrated by procuration. He was made responsible for all the pageantry of that splendid and terrible mock-up involving the entire court, and was so overworked that he died of it.

COCTEAU: The same taste for pomp and circumstance that we found in José-Maria Sert, the great collector and connoisseur of baubles. Perhaps he died of the splendor he worshipped and coveted but could not command. He could never escape from his Ali Baba's cave and treasure-hoard.

ARAGON: But in any case Velázquez was no longer painting toward the end of his career: he was too busy finding lodgings for courtiers. It wore him out and tormented him. Organizing the fictitious wedding of the Sun King shortened the life of one of the greatest painters of all time.

COCTEAU: He was the producer of a tremendous theater. But this Gaspar fascinates me. All these nobles with their wide ruffs or collars seem to have their heads on a platter like St. John the Baptist. What a smile this decapitated fellow is wearing. Gaspar must have been a remarkable person?

ARAGON: He certainly was, but he was always being defeated.

COCTEAU: Now look at his hand: it's as if he were producing evidence of something. He seems to be saying "You don't believe me, but here is the proof."

ARAGON: He was Philip IV's Prime Minister, but fell into disgrace in 1643. One of the finer characteristics of Velázquez is that after

Sir Joshua Reynolds
Portrait of Mr. William James in the Costume of the Dunstable Hunt. 1758

El Greco
Christ Healing the Blind Man.

Jusepe de Ribera
Saint Agnes in Prison. 1641

88

89

90

Diego Velázquez
Portrait of Gaspar de Guzmán.

Diego Velázquez
Portrait of Gaspar de Guzmán.
Detail of Hand.

91

Diego Velázquez
Portrait of a Gentleman. About
1631

Francisco de Zurbarán
St. Bonaventura Praying. 1629

93

School of Fra Angelico
The Annunciation.

the man's disgrace he remained close and friendly with him in spite
of the king. Velázquez was a faithful friend, like Cranach.

COCTEAU: The portrait shows the pride of Gaspar's motto, "The more
you take the more I make."

ARAGON: We have another painter here, a year older than Velázquez.
Zurbarán was born in 1598 and died two years after him.

COCTEAU: This picture reminds me of *The Pilgrims of Emmaus*, the
false Vermeer in Amsterdam.

Francisco de Zurbarán
St. Bonaventura Praying. Page 93

ARAGON: Zurbarán was nothing like Velázquez. Velázquez was the
son of a nobleman and his real name was Silva, Velázquez being his
mother's name; her father was a Portuguese. But Zurbarán was the
son of a plowman and was one himself. Perhaps you remember that
in the middle of the Spanish Pavilion in the International Exhibition
in Paris in 1937, there was a big and rather mad sculpture by Alberto?

COCTEAU: I think I do.

ARAGON: This Alberto was a baker, and his statue was just like
bread. Alberto was a baker again during the war and I saw him quite
recently. He lives in Moscow.

COCTEAU: So Salvador Dali, who claims to have reinvented bread,
is thus in the tradition.

ARAGON: Alberto didn't invent it but kept on making it, even in
stone. Anyway, I met him not long ago in Moscow when a friend,
Nazim Hikmet, took me to his house. Since he became a painter he
paints with astonishing realism.

COCTEAU: Is he painting bread?

ARAGON: No, but things which are exact down to the last hair.

COCTEAU: Now please be careful. We have just been praising Vermeer
for the same exactness. What I want to know is whether this is just
a picture-postcard, or a card addressed from a better world?

ARAGON: Perhaps not a better one. It is a message from another
inferno, rather. Something quite out of the usual. Anyway, Zurbarán
wasn't a baker but a plowman.

COCTEAU: Up in the corner, the angel looks rather like a bather
climbing out of a swimming pool.

ARAGON: As you can see, this composition is based on a contrast
between two halves. On one side we have the world of mysticism,
with a monk praying before the papal crown which is in sharp contrast
to this severe monastic habit. On the other side we have the ordinary
citizens, imposing buildings, and cardinals. The monk is Saint
Bonaventura whom they used to call the Seraphic Doctor: an
extraordinary character who created popes but for a long time refused
a cardinal's hat. There he is, firmly in his thirteenth century, a
completely popular figure. It is quite understandable why our plowman
Zurbarán enjoyed painting him: he painted several other pictures of
Saint Bonaventura and there's even one in the Louvre, if I remember
rightly.

COCTEAU: You'll notice with what love and lavishness the angel and saint are painted, what an expert touch there is in St. Bonaventura's robe and sleeve; and how in contrast the scene in the offing is just sketched in, with those three silhouettes who in no way interest the painter. The background looks like hackwork, mere drudgery, with its dead light. The painter is really fond of his angel and saint and tiara and cloth, but all the rest leaves him cold.

ARAGON: But wait a minute — he is also fond of something else — that enormous shadow that dominates the center of the canvas, separating those two worlds, as well as dividing the world in which that man kneels in prayer from the world of the supernatural.

COCTEAU: The angel is leaning over a wall that is not a real wall. There is a gap in it that is not a real gap, either. The angel is an ectoplasm, only a part of his figure takes shape, with that arm negligently resting on the edge of our real world.

ARAGON: The essence here is shadow. Here we have the hinge uniting our three painters — El Greco, Velázquez, and Ribera — to Zurbarán.

In my view the essential thing about these Spanish masters, and what distinguishes them from the Italian masters, is the predominance of shadow: the shadow around Ribera's angel, the shadow erected like a cross in the middle of Zurbarán's canvas, the blackness so characteristic of El Greco and Velázquez, all that obscure secretiveness and what it was to give to nineteenth-century France when Spanish blackness culminated in Manet.

COCTEAU: I'll take a last look at that little angel whom you compared to the cupids in Picasso's *Verve* series. He is like a little chimney sweep watching a chimney on fire. He is tugging mischievously at the Greco-ish sheet draping the saint. He is about to uncover not only Saint Agnes but Spain itself.

ARAGON: Yes, Spain. It is precisely that dark mischievousness that her great lovers have found in Spain: we become aware of the strange clash between Venice and Toledo, between color and blackness, between Naples and Seville, between Mozart's charming Italian Don Giovanni and Don Juan Tenorio, the heartless Spanish seducer who ended by being boiled in oil.

COCTEAU: Isn't Goya's *Milkmaid* one of the loveliest Renoirs? Isn't the yellow *impasto* of the Maja's corsage one of the richest Manets? I am astonished at the belated scandals in France over works whose original models were quite acceptable in Spain.

ARAGON: Perhaps that is because in Spain nobody saw them as they really were. The Spanish style of painting became more visible when it was transplanted into France.

COCTEAU: That is quite likely. There was nothing intentionally aggressive in Goya's paintings of the royal family. Goya knew that such nobles could never believe they looked ridiculous. They were

Francisco de Goya
The Family of Charles IV

convinced that, being princes, they had no need to look beautiful. The faces in his murderous charade never surprised them, as they were their own. A prince of the blood must be of an essence that is above criticism. I don't think that Goya set out to debunk them. His grotesqueness had its source in that violence that he denounced in the *Caprices* and in the canvases of the Erlanger collection. The violence that royal pride admitted, the violence of the Duchess of Alva, the violence of the mob who dug up her bones to see whether she had been the model for *La Maja* — all that Spanish violence unleashed the violence of the French public, and even Théophile Gautier's when it took the shape of *Olympia* and became Manet's.

Edouard Manet
Olympia

ARAGON: Spain shocks when it is exported — Picasso is an example of that.

COCTEAU: That is possible.

ARAGON: Picasso also suffers from transplantation. Take a very direct Spanish landscape such as *La Huerta:* hang it in the Salon des Indépendants in Paris and it becomes what we call Cubism. To say nothing of his faces which make us wonder whether he had some caricatural intention, as in the Goya portraits you mentioned.

COCTEAU: Picasso is like some rustic squire who insults the Madonna because she is not from his own parish. Picasso embodies that mixture of idolatry and idol-smashing rage which is so typical of the Spaniard and which spurs him on to endless creation and destructiveness. Picasso is the terrorist on his knees, like his fellow countrymen. He is a maze, a labyrinth, and Ariadne's thread, and the Minotaur, a cruel and tender bullfight all on his own. The *corrida* he is busy creating at Vallauris is Muhammad moving the mountain, and as he cannot have his Spain, he makes Spain come to him.

Italian School

School of Fra Angelico
The Annunciation. Page 94

Pinturicchio
Portrait of a Boy. Page 107

ARAGON: If you agree, we can now leave Spain and return to Italy. It means leaving the black and taking to color again.

So here we are, back in Italy. It's always a bit upsetting for me, as I am partly Italian. I had two Italian great-grandmothers and always loved that country which was denied to me for so many years, just as certain words were denied to Eluard. Italy and Spain were out of bounds for me, nearly all my life. My last visit to Italy must have been in the summer of 1928.

To enter Italy and stress its distance from Spain at the very outset, we might glance briefly at this canvas of the school of Fra Angelico — not that it is one of the most outstanding in Dresden, but I think you mentioned only yesterday the extraordinary freshness of his works, which look as if they have scarcely had time to dry. As we are reentering the land of color, let us glance at this ancient source of freshness, but quickly leaving the fourteenth century[14] behind as it is not a period that interests us, to approach the fifteenth and sixteenth centuries. We begin with Pinturicchio, an Umbrian painter who was born in Perugia about 1454 and died at Siena in 1513. This remarkable *Portrait of a Boy* belongs anywhere between those dates.

COCTEAU: It's impossible to imagine a face more thoroughly expressing the contempt of youth for what it cannot understand. This is the face of childhood, firmly shutting in the mysterious treasure that is wasted by adults.

ARAGON: Apart from that, since we described the discovery of landscape as a modern invention in painting, here we can see a Sienese landscape in Pinturicchio's background. This one was done without oil, as for a long time painters refused to use it and Pinturicchio never did.

COCTEAU: Does anyone know this boy's name?

ARAGON: No, it's just called a boy or a youth in the books: the Dresden catalog gives *Ein Knabe,* meaning a boy.

COCTEAU: I repeat that he looks as if he would react violently to anything that might shock his soul.

ARAGON: As I look at him I think of the fate of the man who painted him. Pinturicchio died of neglect and starvation, abandoned by his wife, in 1513. Two centuries later Hobbema died in a hospital and according to the records he was in the paupers' ward. But now let us skip to the masters with whom the sixteenth century opened and developed: Palma Vecchio, Titian, and Tintoretto.

COCTEAU: It was Titian who you said died of . . .

ARAGON: The plague.

COCTEAU: The Black Death, to use its popular name. Yet another.

ARAGON: We are dogged by victims of the plague. Now after Antwerp, London, and Parma we find it in Venice, with Titian. But once in Venice we have to consider the history of Venetian painting on its own, or certain canvases — forgive me for bringing up some works that were not in our first selection — and particularly this Christ and Mary by Giovanni Bellini as a useful contrast. It shows Christ at the tomb, with his mother. The Christ is neither alive nor dead but sits half out of the grave, with his eyes closed. His mother seems to be consoling him.

School of Giovanni Bellini
The Virgin with the Body of
Christ. Page 108

COCTEAU: Here we are faced with the problem of what I call waves and knots in the portrayal of the human body: the waves become knotted, resulting in an architectural work, a dry austerity, a painted line, a lesson in anatomy, like this.

ARAGON: Well, that took us into the workshop of Giovanni Bellini who was an old man then, being born in 1429. This is about 1490 or later, almost 1500 when he was in his sixties and had two apprentices, Giorgione and Titian.

COCTEAU: Apparently Titian suddenly became obsessed with black?

ARAGON: The apprentices soon fell out with their master. Titian left Bellini to join Giorgione who was about his own age and was lucky enough to have his own studio by 1505. He never looked for another master and the two young men painted in the same workshop. Giorgione died quite young in 1510 at the age of thirty-three. Titian completed his friend's paintings; here is one of them, which we did not select, but with your agreement I'll introduce it now. It is what is known as *The Dresden Venus* or *Venus Asleep*, by Giorgione. It is said, though there is some disagreement, that Titian finished it. No doubt its resemblance to Titian's *Recumbent Venus* in the Uffizi has some connection with it. It is interesting to set Giorgione's Venus alongside another that I have added here, a *Venus Reposing* by Palma Vecchio that is rather different.

Giorgione
Venus Asleep. Page 109

Titian
Réclining Venus

Palma Vecchio
Venus Reposing. Page 110

COCTEAU: May I suggest that one has dreamt and the other is dreaming?

ARAGON: Moreover the difference is quite great, as if there were an epoch between the two although they were contemporaneous. But let us consider their forerunner Palma before we come to Titian. Oddly enough, here we have a picture that could easily be taken for German.

COCTEAU: A landscape with very graceful human figures in it.

ARAGON: Yes, it's his *Jacob and Rachel.* The dress is fairly modern. Here Palma is portraying shepherds as he often did.

Palma Vecchio
Jacob and Rachel. Page 111

COCTEAU: But more like courtiers?

ARAGON: Pages in a court of sheep. ... Somehow is it more Swiss than German?

COCTEAU: What a world of difference between those "waves and knots," Tyrolese and psalms, shepherdesses and nudes, and that flayed Christ.

ARAGON: Yet there are only forty years between the painters. There is a great gap between Bellini and Palma Vecchio, but I don't know how to describe the unbridgeable one between Bellini's work and that of Giorgione and Titian.

COCTEAU: I dare say Bellini thought they were quacks.

ARAGON: Yes, he absolutely hated them, which is why shortly after Giorgione's death in 1515 at the time of the Battle of Marignano, when Venice commissioned Titian to paint the Battle of Cadora, Giovanni Bellini had the state's commission withdrawn from his former pupil whom he still pursued with his hatred. Titian had to wait until Bellini's death in 1516 to receive part of his fee. Then he died of the plague himself. The result of all this is that Titian never painted the Battle of Cadora.

COCTEAU: It's the opposite of what happened when David tried to destroy Fragonard.

ARAGON: And for us Titian dominates the whole sixteenth century. Here we have his...

COCTEAU: If you don't mind my interruption, don't you think that Bellini rather anticipates David's *Marat*?

ARAGON: Perhaps — a little.

COCTEAU: And that Ingres's *Turkish Bath* now begins to...

ARAGON: We would do better to contrast that Christ at the Tomb with this young lady in white, holding a little fan or flag in her hand. There she is with her jewels, a vastly different character. There isn't the faintest thing in common between this Titian and the Bellini.

COCTEAU: A plump young woman with a painted face. The sort who listen at keyholes. Nothing austere about her soul.

ARAGON: It happens to be the painter's daughter Lavinia,[15] in her wedding dress. There was at most forty years between this and the Christ and Mary. In the history of painting it is more like two centuries.

COCTEAU: The same astronomical distance as between a Boucher and a David.

ARAGON: Titian died of the plague in Venice in 1576. He is regarded as the greatest of the Venetian school and as having best recorded the splendor of Venice. But personally I am inclined to set a painter of a younger generation, Tintoretto, above him. Tintoretto made a vow to equal Michelangelo's draftsmanship and Titian's color, but you'll remember that Picasso downgraded him as the mere "doorman" of painting.

COCTEAU: It looks as if we are about to fall in love with the same picture. Because we always meet in certain works — as we do in certain places, of an evening, under the plane trees.

ARAGON: Now this is an extraordinary painting, as remote from our plane trees as could be.

Jacques-Louis David
The Death of Marat

Titian
Portrait of a Lady in White.
Page 112

100

COCTEAU: I mentioned the plane trees because I still have in my ears some verses of your new poem, full of the vaults and arches of the planes on the road to Provence. ... But the marvelous work that now delights us looks the very opposite of sweet and simple: what is its title?

ARAGON: *The Deliverance of Arsinoë*. A knight in armor, rescuing two nudes in a boat.

Tintoretto
The Deliverance of Arsinoë.
Page 113

COCTEAU: Not very helpful. We see two naked women in chains, like a modern Andromeda. A style rather like a Doré group that I own. It reminds me of all the details that Rusticiano added to Marco Polo's anecdotes when imprisoned at Genoa. Knights and fine ladies in Arab jails... On the right of this strange canvas a young gondolier prudently averts his eyes from the erotic scene, with all the detachment of Tiepolo's pages leaning over balustrades...

ARAGON: The subject or story was identified early in this century as the rescue of Cleopatra's sister Arsinoë escaping from Alexandria with the help of a knight in armor. The story comes from Lucan's *Pharsalia*, which the painter read in the Italian version. A beauty delivered by a warrior — reminding us of course of Perseus freeing Andromeda. But here we are neither in Egypt nor in Mark Anthony's time, but in Venice itself with an undeniably Venetian boat. You can make anything you like of it: it could just as easily be a scene from *Othello* as from the *Pharsalia,* couldn't it? A scene overlooked by Shakespeare, perhaps? And the young chevalier could easily be one of those Renaissance heroes we find in Stendhal's *Italian Chronicles*. It's pure Stendhal.[16]

COCTEAU: Yes — or pure Tasso, or pure Othello from our friend Yutkeviç's film — and why not pure Pushkin or pure Balzac — when Marsay disguised as a nun climbs over the convent wall on a rope ladder and the thirteen toss the body of the Duchess de Langeais into the sea...

ARAGON: Anyway, it is the high Romanticism of the sixteenth century. Just look at the structure of that tower from which the chained women are escaping: the blocks of stone are carved like diamonds, as in Genoese or Florentine palaces.

COCTEAU: Exactly. Everything that made my tragedy *Renaud and Armide* invisible to critics blinded by Claudel, and a public mad on Giraudoux.

ARAGON: Here we are in the world of Ariosto.

COCTEAU: Pure opera.

ARAGON: As you remarked, the young gondolier is looking at nothing at all, not even the women. He is just doing his job. For him all this is just business as usual.

COCTEAU: He has ferried dozens of that sort in his gondola. And these females won't be the last.

ARAGON: But with Tintoretto we are now observing one of the great moments of painting. The theme of Perseus and Andromeda

Titian
Perseus and Andromeda

was of course a highly topical one for the Venetians, so it was often painted. There is also a *Perseus and Andromeda* by Titian.

COCTEAU: But here, from the hand of a very great painter we find the marvelous bad taste of such artists as Doré and Robida, with the extravagance of a setting in which the sea tosses its mad hair and its foam is like Andromeda's seething dragon with its monstrous jaws in which the planted lance holds Pegasus aloft in the air — in that group which you remember Charles de Noailles once gave me.

ARAGON: You commented on the sea, in a mad frenzy with its frantic hair unloosed: but perhaps that is because we are looking at the black-and-white reproduction.

COCTEAU: In color we shall no doubt find the women very fleshy, not very nuanced or modulated, with a deliberate contrast between the ironclad man and the female forms in nothing but their chains.

ARAGON: Now here it is, in color.

COCTEAU: The gondolier seems to be the only realistic note in that demented orchestra.

Tintoretto
Portrait of an Old and a Young
Man. Page 114

ARAGON: Yet with Tintoretto we have one of the outstanding realists of the sixteenth century. There is sufficient proof in that other canvas we selected, the *Portrait of an Old and a Young Man.*

COCTEAU: We cannot leave those two nudes and their knight without stressing that it is the kind of painting that would have delighted the Surrealists, when your group was in full swing.

ARAGON: If only they knew how to look at it.

COCTEAU: You are more royalist than the king. But it could have been a collage or montage by Max Ernst.

ARAGON: But I think the madness of that sea is different from what Ernst's or our madness was.

COCTEAU: Possibly, but the unreal realism of this work and its very unusual contrasts do relate it to Surrealism.

ARAGON: Yes, but it is surprising that the painter you are calling surrealist is also the realist who painted this dual portrait.

COCTEAU: Not so fast! One might well think that the young man here is telling the old man things that he is not used to hearing about. Perhaps the young man is telling him all about modern painting...

ARAGON: You could be all the more right as the old man is certainly Tintoretto himself. And if the young man is not El Greco, then he is one of his contemporaries such as the young Palma, or Malombra, or Contarini. We may compare this masterpiece with the *Portrait of the Artist with His Grandson* in the Vienna Museum, which is attributed to him but could be the work of his daughter Marietta. The composition is similar but here Tintoretto is ten of fifteen years older and the young man four or five years younger. There is an enormous difference in their craftsmanship and realism.

It is remarkable that this same painter discovered modern warfare. The "Romantic" of the *Arsinoë* and the great portraits was also the artist of the *Defense of Brescia,* the *Battle of Riva,* the *Fall of Parma,* the *Taking of Gallipoli* and that of *Pavia* and *Zara,* and also the *Battle on the Adige* and the *Battle on the Taro* — all pictures in which the new machines of war are shown in action with astonishing power. For me this is the summit of Italian painting, even if we count Bassano and Veronese, after which there is nothing to be said for a century or perhaps forever. For the Italian seventeenth century failed to achieve the greatness of the Flemish or the Dutch, and we have to wait until the eighteenth before finding painters who can move our passions, though naturally in a different way. I'll be accused of ignoring Caravaggio, no doubt; but he was a contemporary of Tintoretto and survived him by almost fifteen years.

COCTEAU: There is also something of Delacroix — Monsieur Lacroix as George Sand called him — forgive me but I wanted to say something more about the Tintoretto.

ARAGON: Of course.

COCTEAU: I was going to say that it recalls Delacroix's *Dante's Barque.* But where was this Tintoretto kept? Where was it hung, how did people see it? That's what I want to know.

ARAGON: We have no account of such details. To understand them we should need to look at a few pages in Stendhal's *Vittoria Accoramboni.*

COCTEAU: Or Tasso?

ARAGON: I think that would explain less. Tintoretto would help us to explain Tasso; but to explain Tintoretto I think we would have to turn to Stendhal, to the men in his *Italian Chronicles* who are the people we are talking about.

COCTEAU: Perhaps this canvas suffers in the same way as those in which Hieronymus Bosch illustrated anecdotes that everyone knew by heart but that we no longer know now. No doubt the charm of that gondola, knights, and nudes, arises from their being like some object that is only mysterious because we no longer know what it is for, what is its use. It has strayed out of reality into the unreal.

ARAGON: Yes, but whatever Lucan's account may be, I am sure that nobody ever said before we did that the prison or tower has diamond-shaped walls, or that the women's rescuers floated on a sea of white horses' manes.

COCTEAU: A shock of white hair. The diamond-faceted wall recalls the diamond-fronted house in Marseilles that was destroyed by the Germans, in the slums of the Vieux-Port. It is the height of romanticism. One senses that the young man lifting his oar from the rowlock will someday be rowing Lord Byron, and a couple composed of the bearded young lady Alfred de Musset and the skirted young man George Sand, as well as Cambridge undergraduates with a volume of Keats under their arm.

ARAGON: And of course Pushkin. Not long ago you mentioned the poem I read to you (but heaven knows what our readers would make of it) about that square with its plane trees in the evening: well, it also contained a stanza about the Adriatic.

COCTEAU: Yes, I remember that.

ARAGON: Well, don't tell anyone, but it was translated from Pushkin, at least in my head, for it contains the first line of *Eugene Onegin.*

COCTEAU: One has the right to take over texts that intrude into one's mind. As Pushkin is untranslatable your poem gives an equivalent. His breath invades you and takes a familiar shape in my mind.

ARAGON: But we must come to the Italian eighteenth century now.

COCTEAU: Here we have Piazzetta, 1682–1754. His *Young Standard-Bearer* is a brother of our Gavroche on the barricades. Delacroix and Courbet would fit him into some Commune incident.

ARAGON: There's also a hint of David here.

COCTEAU: Yes, but a David by Courbet. He doesn't jeer but is quite serious and well behaved. But you are right — he is closer to David than to Gavroche.

ARAGON: There's a curiously close relationship between the texture of the banner and the boy's face.

COCTEAU: He is holding himself in reserve for some possible action. You feel that if there were any violence he would dash in enthusiastically, waving his banner under a hail of shot. Or he could well be at some religious festival, Corpus Christi with holy wafers and girls tossing rose-petals. Which goes to show that a picture's "subject" is of no great importance, as everyone adapts it to his own private world and memories.

ARAGON: I am not so sure. It makes me think rather of the children of the great Revolution, because of the casualness of the uniform. He is watching some spectacle or procession go by, and is impressed. You see that hand grasping the standard at the top? You can feel his finger tightening on the cloth.

In any case we can take him as the usher opening the Italian eighteenth century.

COCTEAU: And in him I hail an ancestor of Manet's *Fife Player.*

ARAGON: Yes, he is very close to our own French style. Close to many French things and introducing — exactly what? Something that is decidedly quite remote from him, from the child represented here, and yet quite close to Piazzetta.

COCTEAU: Now the curtain of his banner lifts to reveal an unusual sight. We see a turmoil of men and beasts, horses and sea-shells and conches and nudes and dolphins with children riding on them and draperies and waves. A Bouguereau seen through the Douanier Rousseau's imagination. His naive eye transfigured a daub into a splendid masterpiece.

ARAGON: It is *The Triumph of Amphitrite* by Giovanni Battista Tiepolo. I wonder why we chose it?

Giovanni Battista Piazzetta
A Young Standard-Bearer.
Page 115

Edouard Manet
The Fife Player

Giovanni Battista Tiepolo
The Triumph of Amphitrite.
Page 116

COCTEAU: It is like Racine's "Speech of Theramenes." We kept it in because of that mysterious razor's edge between the worthless and the sublime. The strip of drapery that replaced your young David's sling is lifted to reveal a theatrical climax. I should like to see it in color — do we have it?

ARAGON: I think so.

COCTEAU: Have a look. It's a long wide canvas.

ARAGON: I can't find it here. Yes, here it is. (He finds the plate and Cocteau fits it into the projector.)

COCTEAU: The colors, also, are almost repulsive, with the instinctive self-confidence of genius. The painter does not question himself at all. Nothing can hold him back. He flings himself headlong into danger. The result is a fantastic painting.

ARAGON: Well, it is certainly on the fringe of taste. With Tiepolo we are entering an entirely new phase of Venetian painting. It is no longer Othello's Venice, but Casanova's.

COCTEAU: Was Piazzetta also a Venetian, as his name suggests?

ARAGON: Yes, but a Venetian who had spent some time in Bologna. The Bolognese realists were a prelude to the new Venetian carnival. In the seventeenth century Caravaggio's light took refuge in Bologna, in that Bolognese realism of which the best exponent was Guercino. Piazzetta was his pupil and is said to be the link between Veronese and Tiepolo. Now we are back in Venice with Tiepolo's picture — and with his brother-in-law Francesco Guardi. (He places the photograph of a Guardi next to the Tiepolo.)

COCTEAU (still looking at the colored Tiepolo): The birth of the pearl in the oyster. A graceful sickness of art. A treasure from the depths.

ARAGON: It's odd that this mythological image should have been born by the Adriatic.

COCTEAU: This Tiepolo reminds one of the nuptial hamper that Neptune gave to the doge after he threw his ring into the Adriatic. (He takes up the Guardi.)

ARAGON: Now we are in the Piazza San Marco, facing the great double stairway of the Scuola di San Marco. The light is behind us. A thousand flashes pick out the men's white collars and wigs, the white robes and copes of the ladies, the halberts of the guards. Some important public ceremony is being held in the Most Serene Republic.

COCTEAU: I saw this picture recently in the Ashmolean in Oxford. With such lavish detail as this, one wonders how the man had the patience to paint the same thing twice over. Yet they tell me that there are three or four canvases of the same scene. Guardi painted them on commission and sold them on the Piazza San Marco, like a photographer.

ARAGON: It is *Pope Pius VI Blessing the Venetians from the Scuola di San Marco.* Guardi was by far the most expensive and so the most "successful" painter of his day. He was Canaletto's pupil.

COCTEAU: Then perhaps he had pupils who made copies of the

Francesco Guardi
Pope Pius VI Blessing the Venetians from the Scuola di San Marco. Page 117

Francesco Guardi
Pope Pius VI Blessing the Crowd in the Piazza in Front of St. John and St. Paul

original work. The Venetian painters never had our self-importance and saw nothing undignified in having a team of assistants.

ARAGON: Either explanation is possible – or both are. We saw that with El Greco, who made three copies of his *Christ Healing the Blind Man.*

COCTEAU: When the king was disturbed by El Greco's boldness he had him watched by his sculptor Pompea Leone, to keep him in check. There are several versions of *The Martyrdom of St. Julian* and the genuine one, which the experts took for a forgery, is in J.-M.Sert's collection. The young page in it is wearing modern dress. El Greco never heard the last of that commission, the king finding the legs too long, and the Pope finding the angels' wings too short. El Greco was badgered by a tribunal which prevented him from painting in his own way.

ARAGON: The problem you raise about Guardi is compounded with another, as we are now coming to a painter who was (so to speak) not one man but two. For there are two Canalettos: the old Antonio Canal, and his nephew Bernardo Bellotto known as the Saxon Canaletto. They signed with the same name. Of course there's a pile of Bellottos in Dresden, but how can one help preferring old Antonio? Just look at this.

Canaletto
The Piazza in Front of
San Giacomo di Rialto in Venice.
Page 118

COCTEAU: Oh – here we have one of those paintings we both feel the same about. That Venetian square – that part in the shade there, and under the arcades, and that pink wall – for I'm sure it must be pink and look, down there, some painters arguing over prices. Do we only have it in black-and-white?

ARAGON: It is wonderful. Yes, we have it in color as well. (They look at the colored reproduction on the screen.)

COCTEAU: Can't we add it to the few exceptional works that impress us more than the rest?

ARAGON: It is quite obvious that this was by Guardi's master, Giovanni Antonio Canal, the elder Canaletto.

Jan Vermeer van Delft
View of the Town of Delft

COCTEAU: It reminds me of the pink house by Vermeer, which Proust's Bergotte was gazing at as he died.[17]

ARAGON: Now, on the pink wall you enthused about at the same time as the little figures down below, you can see some clothes hung out to dry between the church section and the part that has a little pavilion built on top of it.

COCTEAU: I really love this scene. It's as tender as a cheek – you feel like kissing it.

ARAGON: It's astonishing how, when you saw it in black-and-white, you said it must be pink; then when we showed the colored slide we found a building entirely and surprisingly all that color, a rosy pink. You take that intuition for granted, you don't even notice it. You saw the Canaletto as pink, and so it turned out to be. Very pink. The best comment we can make on this Canaletto is to set it politely alongside a Bellotto: for instance, this *Neustädter Market in Dresden,* by Antonio's nephew. It's like leaving Italy in a painter's luggage. ...

Bernardo Bellotto
The Neustädter Market. Page 119

Pinturicchio
Portrait of a Boy. About 1481–83

School of Giovanni Bellini
The Virgin with the Body of Christ.

Giorgione
Venus Asleep.

109

Palma Vecchio
Venus Reposing.

Palma Vecchio
Jacob and Rachel.

111

Titian
Portrait of a Lady in White.
About 1555

Tintoretto
The Deliverance of Arsinoë.
After 1560

Tintoretto
Portrait of an Old and a Young Man.

Giovanni Battista Piazzetta
A Young Standard-Bearer. About 1620—25

114

Giovanni Battista Tiepolo
The Triumph of Amphitrite.
About 1740

116

Francesco Guardi
Pope Pius VI Blessing the Venetians
from the Scuola di San Marco.
1782

Bernardo Bellotto
The Neustädter Market. 1750

Canaletto
*The Piazza in Front of San
Giacomo di Rialto in Venice.*
Before 1730

Nicolas Poussin
Narcissus.

Claude Lorrain
*Coast Scene with Acis and
Galatea.* 1657

121

Antoine Watteau
A Garden Party.

French School

ARAGON: Here we are in France at last, having approached it through Italy. We have not included any French primitive painting in our selection. We begin with our seventeenth century which owes nothing to the North nor to Flanders or Spain, but which has Italianate traditions. The most typically French of these painters, Nicolas Poussin, actually lived in Italy. We chose this rather unusual picture of his, *Narcissus.*

Nicolas Poussin
Narcissus. Page 120

COCTEAU: Here the figures appear more important than the setting. It is above all a theatrical scene. Narcissus hasn't just a walk-on part, he is the star. Echo, the nymph, is being transformed into a rock. She is a mime, an actress who is part of the scenery, a female "prop" in the landscape. But this time the figures of Narcissus and Echo have not been added by a second painter's hand.

ARAGON: We find ourselves in the Roman conception of nature, with fauns running across the background. Here we are in that countryside that young French artists sought when they went to the School in Rome.[18]

COCTEAU: So did young Germans. There was young Goethe lolling among the ruins on a Louis-Quinze sofa.

ARAGON: A striking element here is the curious likeness between this Roman landscape and French landscape, whether it was painted in France or in Italy. It is the landscape of both Poussin and Corot. After all, this is Ville d'Avray.

COCTEAU: Yes, Ville d'Avray — you have put your finger on the essential point. The mythology is also familiar to us because of those inns at Barbizon. The rocks are those artificial-looking rocks in the Forest of Fontainebleau, the sandstone blocks left there by the receding sea. So the lady is being changed into a Fontainebleau rock, with the hound of a terracotta huntress.

ARAGON: It's odd that we should have two French painters associated with Roman landscape in the same period and whose names are always mentioned together, although they are poles apart. I mean Claude Gellée, variously known as Claude Lorrain, or Le Lorrain, or just Claude; and Nicolas Poussin. You asked me to retain this Claude.

Claude Lorrain
Coast Scene with Acis and Galatea.
Page 121

COCTEAU: Yes, the Galatea one.

ARAGON: The *Coast Scene with Acis and Galatea,* as it is called. The landscape in this one is of a different character. Here we have an artist who was essentially a landscape painter. He introduces myth and fable into landscape as Poussin did, but with an unusual lightness of touch, an almost throwaway manner.

COCTEAU: In the far distance you can see Polyphemus hiding among the trees, as in those puzzle-pictures in which you have to find the hunter. One doesn't notice him at first sight, up in the right-hand corner.

ARAGON: He is hidden away up there like some trivial detail, but the story goes that he was out to kill the young and handsome Acis (whom we see there under the tent) out of jealousy for the nymph Galatea. It is interesting that Claude should have tried this theme, as it was also handled by Poussin. Have you seen Poussin's version in Madrid? The main difference is that Poussin includes no seascape, but sets the story in the Roman countryside among the hills, where the romance of Galatea and Acis was supposed to have happened, and the presence of the jealous Cyclops above them, preparing to hurl his rock, is much more sinister than in Claude's idyllic scene.

But the story was taken much farther as regards the presence of Polyphemus in a canvas by Watteau, of which only an engraving has survived.

COCTEAU: You astonish me.

ARAGON: Yes, Watteau took up the same subject, but instead of Claude's sea and Poussin's enormous valley, he set the story in a little French dale.

COCTEAU: In a park?

ARAGON: Not quite: the setting is very rustic, close to French peasant life.

COCTEAU: Are the figures dressed as in Watteau's time?

ARAGON: No, they are naked. It's a mythological painting, by Watteau. Polyphemus is confused with the rocks and foliage, up above, and his figure in black-and-white is suspended in the air as if he himself is about to be hurled like a rock on the shepherd Acis. There's a print of it in this book, here...

COCTEAU (looking): Yes, he is integrated into the landscape. He is as rocklike as the nymph Echo in that painting of Narcissus we looked at.

ARAGON: Yes. Anyone might think that we unconsciously selected our Claude and Poussin in such a way as to reach Watteau more easily. Well, here we are now, really at home.

COCTEAU: With Watteau we have a prodigy comparable to Vermeer. All that gracefulness has a terrifying relief about it. The wig-powder cloudiness predicts the storm to come. A sadistic charm.

ARAGON: What has happened is that in leaving Italy for good, we rediscover Flanders. Watteau's landscape is contemporary with Hobbema's, but he peoples it with his own characters who are the particular innovation of French painting. He introduced the Italian Commedia dell'Arte into Flemish landscapes. Of the two pictures we have chosen, the one with figures on a stone bench is certainly very fine, but the other, *A Garden Party*,[19] has a really exhilarating part, that bit of landscape on the left.

COCTEAU: What strikes me is the amount of suppressed violence in that hazy atmosphere, the powerful grip underlying that elegance — a grace that relates to the darker side of Courbet. The enormous hips on that statue remind one of the *Demoiselles de la Seine.*

ARAGON: Believe it or not, another painter has offered an appreciation of this canvas — none other than Renoir himself. He said: "In Dresden there's a Watteau with a marvelous landscape in it." We can see for ourselves how and why he must have liked it.

COCTEAU: Renoir's olive trees and bathing nymphs evoke *L'Après-Midi d'un Faune* better than Manet's illustrations, their "light incarnate shimmering in the air." You would think that Mallarmé was interpreting a scene painted by Renoir on one of those delightful little canvases in the Alec Weisweiller collection.

ARAGON: The difference between the two scenes is that in this one the landscape really dominates the figures.

COCTEAU: But there is also a trap for the unwary. As in the case of Mozart, one can easily imagine the thousands of ignorant people who take Watteau for a frivolous artist, a comic-opera painter: but I wonder whether you remember how our slow-witted Derain fainted in front of *Gersaint's Signboard* in the Musée d'Art Moderne? He came up the staircase very fast, glanced at the picture, felt the familiar queasiness one has at the top of a ladder, then fainted on a bench. I rather like that story. Derain the "rude mechanical" suddenly feeling out of sorts as if the gods of Olympus had suddenly appeared in a cloud of wig-powder.

ARAGON: Perhaps. There is a sort of *Watteauesque* France, just as I said there is a Tintoretto's Italy. On the whole Watteau is my favorite French painter, and for many reasons. Do you know that extraordinary work, the album of Watteau's drawings engraved by Boucher?

COCTEAU: Of course.

ARAGON: Because in it one suddenly sees his draftsmanship and the personalities he later painted into his pictures. You see them exactly as he did, for instance the Italian actors of the Hôtel de Bourgogne, just as they were in real life before taking on the unrealness of color.

COCTEAU: In black and red chalk, aren't they?

ARAGON: Yes, drawings of absolute precision, people you really meet, far more accurate than Daumier, for instance, and I'm not saying that lightly: they are really people as you see them at work, like Daumier's laundry maids, or caught in a daydream like his people in a railway carriage.

COCTEAU: Watteau got the vicar of Saint-Maur to pose for his *Gilles.* He refused to kiss the crucifix on his death-bed and said "Fetch me one I can kiss, this one is in very bad taste." This all corresponds to the iron hand in the velvet glove.

ARAGON: Watteau also did some war scenes. I mention this because I was thinking of Tintoretto: there are some war scenes by Watteau, who was a witness or reporter, among other things. When Watteau was on his way home from Paris, traveling on foot at the time of the battle of Malplaquet, he saw the defeat of the French army and recorded the retreat. In his drawings and several paintings he interpreted the scenes of disorder, the evacuations, halts, temporary camps. I say interpreted or transposed because when I look at Watteau's garden parties and amorous picnics it always strikes me that those people are not merely enjoying an outing but have come together by chance. They are people who were bound for somewhere else but found themselves in a park among the statues like the one you mentioned earlier on. Just look at that man near the statue which no doubt represents a river, for she is leaning on a conch behind her: just look at his townsman's surprise at wandering into this estate by accident. The owners have fled and the intruders have nothing better to do than drink the burgundy left in the cellars, before the German troops overtake them.

COCTEAU: Yes, they are like people coming together as a result of a railway accident, or during a halt or bombardment when they have left their cars on the road.

ARAGON: So they are having a picnic on a bench, but certainly not only for the fun of it.

COCTEAU: What strikes me about Watteau is how he restores its medieval meaning to the word "charm," an enchantment of magic spell.

ARAGON: A *charme* in the sense that Valéry used in the plural, *charmes*. But we must let him sleep in his graveyard by the sea...

COCTEAU: In Watteau there's not the slightest hint of some genteel little finger sticking up in the air: but a good firm grip.

ARAGON: Yes, those people are not there just for their amusement.

COCTEAU: Their frills and flounces are their armor, they are mailed in satins.

ARAGON: And just look at those trees — not just shady walks in parks, but the ash groves around Valenciennes.

COCTEAU: When you're in front of a masterpiece there's not much point in thinking; but if I had to think it would be about Rimbaud, his little actors and actresses with their ribbons and rosettes.

ARAGON: Of course. That is no accident as Rimbaud and Watteau came from the same parts.

COCTEAU: So there you are.

ARAGON: It's no distance, from Charleville to Valenciennes.

COCTEAU: And the little provincial stages with strolling players, the marvelous red barn shows in smoke-blue scenery...

ARAGON: And the adolescent Rimbaud mooning through this little dell with its dancing sunbeams, on his way to meet Gilles. ...

COCTEAU: They'd be playing *The Two Little Orphans* with four or five actors and canvas trees fastened to fishing-nets...

ARAGON: And don't forget Rimbaud's pools and ponds. Look, this isn't exactly a lake, but exactly what Rimbaud meant by a pond...

COCTEAU: We are both easily hooked by poet-painters and painter-poets. We cannot help it. Nothing can stop us. The poetry of painting bewitches both of us. And very soon when we come to the Impressionists we'll again be caught by some painting that is a poem.

ARAGON: Yes — but first we have to finish our eighteenth century.

COCTEAU: A whole Age of the Pharaohs glimpsed through windows, or in glass cases, glass sarcophagi.

ARAGON: Yes. We can choose one painter to represent them all — Maurice Quentin de La Tour, and just one portrait, his *Maréchal de Saxe.*

Maurice Quentin de La Tour
Count Maurice of Saxony,
Marshal of France. Page 131

COCTEAU: The Field-Marshal is inspecting our epoch from behind his sheet of glass. The glass prevents the powder from dropping off his hair, his sleeve, his cheeks. The Henri de Rothschild family owned a splendid La Tour, *The Man in Gray.* Every time a bus passed through the Faubourg Saint-Honoré a bit of gold dust or pastel fell off it. Instead of hanging it somewhere else, they asked the Prefect of Police to change the bus-route — and he did.

ARAGON: Most of La Tour's pastels are at Saint-Quentin, and that means quite a crowd, a society of their own.

COCTEAU: They stare at us like Peeping Toms spying through one-way mirrors. They think we don't know that they are watching us.

ARAGON: Just imagine all those fine ladies and middle-class belles and princesses and actresses, down there at Saint-Quentin. Madame de Pompadour and all the rest. They used to send pupils from the drawing schools to copy La Tour, until it was decided to stop because it seemed unsafe to let young people loose among the disturbing females of a disturbing epoch. But I'm inclined to think that the young men regarded them as something like madonnas, for to tell the truth we can no longer understand the eighteenth-century woman. They rarely have the kind of charm that people can understand nowadays. But I must say that we can almost rediscover that charm in this remarkable cinema pinup which I have just unearthed from our pile of photographs. Just look at her — could anyone have more charm than this Viennese *Chocolate-Girl?*

Jean-Etienne Liotard
The Chocolate-Girl. Page 132

COCTEAU: Liotard, the artist we are about to discuss, painted a portrait of Madame d'Epinay reclining on a divan in Persian costume. Her outfit would harmonize very well with Rousseau's Armenian dress, which he wore for less elegant reasons.

ARAGON: Liotard deserves far greater recognition than he has been given.

COCTEAU: The astonishing Liotard reminds me of Paul Léautaud whom he resembles in both name and appearance, except in the portrait we have here in which he is wearing a beard. Sometimes he makes himself look like a porter at his window. Here he is bearded and disguised as a Turk. But you just said something that throws light on this getup, as this queer pastelist left Geneva and went to Constantinople with an Englishman.

Jean-Etienne Liotard
Self-Portrait in Turkish Costume.
Page 133

ARAGON: He is usually thought of as being Swiss, but he was only born in Switzerland by chance.

COCTEAU: Did he also die there?

ARAGON: He was born there and died there, but he was the son of someone from Montélimar who had become a refugee in Switzerland for political reasons.

COCTEAU: This pastel has all the creamy unctuousness of oils.

ARAGON: This places him directly after La Tour. La Tour and Liotard had a very different fate...

COCTEAU: Off and on, Liotard wore a beard or was close-shaven. Here he has that fuzzy affair with thousands of close curls — the birds could nest in it as in the case of some of Edward Lear's nonsense characters.

ARAGON: This beard looks rather artificial.

COCTEAU: Yes, he just "wears" his beard, like Proust who was always chopping and changing with his. When Proust died he had that Carnot or Captain Cuttle style of beard. I knew him clean-shaven, as he was in the portrait by Jacques-Emile Blanche. You could count every hair in Liotard's beard — he always used pastel like a miniaturist.

ARAGON: As it happens, that Swiss who wasn't Swiss was the last French painter of the eighteenth century. He died just a month before the fall of the Bastille.

COCTEAU: Yes — what a farewell to all that, it was.

ARAGON: It was that century's way of saying good-bye. And now there is nothing to stop us from skipping the whole school of David, Delacroix, and Géricault, so as to land in the distant outcome of it all, the modern phase of painting which opens with Manet. Everything after that Spanish shadow was pointing toward Manet.

Edouard Manet
Lady in a Pink Dress. Page 134

Edgar Degas
Lady with Binoculars. Page 135

COCTEAU: With this portrait, *Lady in a Pink Dress,* we are in Manet's Franco-Spanish period. This lady is the very image of those comfortable *bourgeoises* sitting at their drawing-room window in Paris to watch the Spanish *corrida.* This other portrait, the *Lady with Binoculars* by Degas is on the fringe of Impressionism: but more constructive, it shows her watching the Auteuil races with her glasses. You know how Degas painted? He used to enlarge photographs and paint his first sketches on faint proofs. Then he went on to paint his picture without using the photographs. Many of the Impressionists did the same thing. This explains the stiff postures of some of their figures and the stance of this woman who looks as if she had just walked out of the poem you read to me the other day. She belongs to our grandmothers' time, but also reminds me of our mothers with their muffs and toques and astrakhan jackets.

ARAGON: As for Degas, do you remember how after the 1914—18 war we were suddenly faced with the great Degas sale, when all the works from his studio were made public? No painter ever impressed me so much, even though Degas was never my favorite: but perhaps

it was the first time I ever saw an artist's entire work all at once,
in all its variety from the *Semiramis* which is now in the Louvre, to the
ballet dancers and laundry maids and women ironing, and all the rest.
But perhaps what was missing was this woman here, with her binoculars.

COCTEAU: Her race-glasses.

ARAGON: She is the type of woman just after Constantin Guys,
something quite near to us, our mothers' generation.

COCTEAU: No, I insist — our grandmothers'.

ARAGON: And after all there is a great difference between them
and that lady in pink, who all the same has the unexpected charm...

COCTEAU: Of a Goya?

ARAGON: Of a pink and black Goya. But we find something of Spain
again in that lady's field-glasses.

COCTEAU: Anna Karenina at the races.

ARAGON: Here we are more thoroughly in France, more totally in
Paris. We can pass from her directly to the opera with this
characteristic Degas. This *Two Dancers* has all his charm, everything
that requires no commentary, not because everything has been
said but because there is too much to say.

Edgar Degas
Two Dancers. Page 136

COCTEAU: Two Japanese chrysanthemums. Here we have that Japanese
touch that we also feel in Vuillard. It's odd to think of Pierre Loti
as a forerunner of Impressionism.

ARAGON: Against those two dancers we can set these two women of
Toulouse-Lautrec's. They are not dancing, but relaxing. Lautrec
probably found them in one of his haunts near the Bibliothèque Nationale.
These women are played out, no longer young or beautiful but with
all the presence that Degas managed to extract from the glow of the
footlights: only here it is the glow of life that has taken over.

Henri de Toulouse-Lautrec
Two Women-Friends. Page 137

COCTEAU: And you'll notice how we are back to the same old
problem, how the ugly females become beautiful thanks to whatever
was beautiful in Lautrec himself, although he was a freak. An ugly
Lautrec and an ugly woman together create a painting as fresh as a
bouquet of April flowers.

ARAGON: Here we have bouquet and garden, all the exoticism of
Paris.

COCTEAU: Lautrec's picture heralds Vuillard: indeed he anticipates
the Fauves even more than Bonnard did.

ARAGON: Alongside these "chrysanthemums" let us put something
quite unlike them, these other two women, the Tahitian *vahinés*.
Now we are in the world of Gauguin. The strange thing here is how
exoticism can take the place of madness.

Paul Gauguin
Two Tahitian Women. Page 138

COCTEAU: In our time we have seen so many albums of them, and
photographers have brought back so many photographs of such women,
that in the end all we can see is that Gauguin was mad about accuracy.

ARAGON: Yes, we hardly remember which came first, the cameraman
or Gauguin.

COCTEAU: The first time I ever saw some Gauguins was in photographs. The photography solidified and sculpted them, gave them an extra dimension. Black-and-white flatters his work, giving it more plastic relief.

ARAGON: After seeing a typical Lautrec, a typical Degas, and a typical Gauguin, now we suddenly pass to an untypical Renoir, *Captain Darras.*

COCTEAU: Enter the captain with a rolling of drums. Are you showing me a character from *Les Mariés de la Tour Eiffel?*

ARAGON: A captain complete with *Légion d'Honneur* and gongs, no doubt earned on colonial service.

COCTEAU: And who could have decorated Van Gogh's *Zouave* with his own hands.

ARAGON: His face is haggard as a result of services rendered to the army and the motherland. He has an imposing armchair, though there's not much of it to be seen.

COCTEAU: You feel that he might have been the one who declared "A general never yields to the enemy or the evidence."

ARAGON: He is no doubt a half-pay captain who has only dressed up in his uniform to pose for Monsieur Renoir. And it's very fine: a splendid picture and a quite unique Renoir.

COCTEAU: It's a forecast of the Dreyfus affair and the numerous families, the great Jewish clans that Renoir was to paint in their salons: the Rothschilds, the Ephrussis.

ARAGON: It would be worthwhile going to Dresden if only to visit this gentleman.

COCTEAU: Absolutely. This is as unexpected as seeing Vollard dressed as a toreador. We are so used to Renoir's nubile young ladies.

ARAGON: It would not surprise me if this retired captain dyed his hair in order to look younger.

COCTEAU: And this fine soldier, as Mallarmé put it [in one of his *Petits Airs*]: "Proud (although I shouldn't say so)/To feel how the homefires glow/ In these military trews...

ARAGON: ...Blushing bloody on my thews." We have Van Gogh's[20] *Zouave,* Renoir's captain, Mallarmé's fire-eater: but there is also Charles Cros's naval officer, "Here comes the naval officer, with his black side-whiskers."

COCTEAU: Anyhow, it is a magnificent painting: Renoir couldn't help making a magnificent painting, his pictures grow as naturally as plants and flowers. He is the most anti-intellectual of painters, yet in this one there's a certain intellectual strength such as we also find in the one of Vollard as a toreador. It is a humorous painting, but I see it as a beautiful peony. I must stress that we are not concerned with the captain but with Renoir, and that the painter is always making his self-portrait, whether he is painting a captain or an anemone.

ARAGON: As with Flaubert and Madame Bovary: "The captain is me."

Maurice Quentin de La Tour
Count Maurice of Saxony,
Marshal of France.

Jean-Etienne Liotard
The Chocolate-Girl. 1743—45

Jean-Etienne Liotard
Self-Portrait in Turkish Costume.

Edouard Manet
Lady in a Pink Dress. 1881

Edgar Degas
Lady with Binoculars.

Edgar Degas
Two Dancers. About 1898

Henri de Toulouse-Lautrec
Two Women-Friends. 1895

137

Paul Gauguin
Two Tahitian Women. 1892

Auguste Renoir
Portrait of Captain Darras. 1871

Claude Monet
A Bend in the Seine near Lava-
court. 1879

Vincent van Gogh
Still Life with Pears. 1898/99

142

COCTEAU: A splendid canvas, which could easily catch us out. We could have said that we were out of luck and that there isn't a real Renoir in Dresden — but this is a very real Renoir. To make a pun, this is *Re-noir* humor, not black humor but red humor.

ARAGON: After this real Renoir we are now coming to a real Impressionist landscape.

COCTEAU: So it is: but this Claude Monet rather disturbs me.

ARAGON: This view of the Seine by Monet could easily be mistaken for a Pissarro or a Sisley. It's the kind of painting that could never have existed before the Impressionists came along. But — as you were saying about the Impressionists yesterday — it now looks to us like a bit of color photography.

COCTEAU: While turning their backs on photography, they produced the most astonishing photographs.

ARAGON: Because they were creating a kind of photography that had not yet come into existence.

COCTEAU: It's hard to believe that (if I've got it right) Diderot said that you have to stand a good distance away from a Chardin to see what it is supposed to represent, yet nowadays we regard Chardin as being very exact indeed. According to Diderot, you had to stand a good meter away in order to see what he was driving at. Perhaps, in his day, a Chardin was like one of those Impressionist canvases that Misia Sert's snobbish friends used to hang upside down so as to make fun of Bonnard and her at the same time.

ARAGON: There's no end to it. My mother used to paint pictures in the impressionist style. Only in secret, though, in case people would think she was mad, and when I was a boy she educated me surreptitiously by making me look at the Impressionists. Then one day she wept when she found some Cubist prints in my room, and said, "Watch out, that is the road to ruin!"

COCTEAU: All the bad roads lead to Rome. Now we can say good-bye to Claude Monet in the same way as the director of the Aix-en-Provence Museum did to Picasso, when he said "Goodbye, Mister Pissarro, I am glad to have been able to show you around the museum." We can say "Good-bye, Mister Pissarro" to Mister Monet.

ARAGON: We have not quite finished with him yet.

COCTEAU: Far from it. Now we have a picture that takes our breath away, it's such a masterpiece, a quite inexplicable masterpiece. We can only wonder why it is a work of genius. Nothing but a jar, his *Still Life with Peaches,* a jar full of the foetuses of peaches. The jar and the peaches are standing on a marble-topped table that reflects part of the glass, and the whole thing is set against a rather nondescript background, and that is all — yet we have a work of genius and cannot explain why. Here we have that genius that defies analysis, the *mystery* we have been discussing throughout these dialogues. But I'll let you take over because I feel that with this jar we

Claude Monet
A Bend in the Seine near Lavacourt. Page 140

Claude Monet
Still Life with Peaches. Page 141

find a more significant mystery than we did in Vermeer. You just showed me the black-and-white slide. Now that I see it in color, instead of losing anything it is even better. Now the marble leaps alive with light, the fruit on the table glows like human cheeks and croups or the hips of Venus, while the fruit in the jar assumes a ghostly pallor. It is a marvel, a miracle. I now pass you the microphone because this is a painting which...

ARAGON: Yes, it is really overwhelming, but impossible to say why. This is a painting in a class of its own, radiating a mysterious feeling of life. Through this Monet we suddenly become aware of the triumph of the still life at the dawn of this century, after the domination of Impressionist landscape. I have no idea why this work is so compelling: you call it a triumph and of course it is better in color; yet this picture is one of those cases when we have to see the black and colored versions side by side in order to grasp it: one helps the other, they complete each other. If you look at the fruit in the jar in both photographs, and then take the colored one by itself, you will see that the fruit is then more "photographic" than in the monochrome version.

COCTEAU: They are the foetuses of fruit, ghosts of fruit, they look dead, haunting.

ARAGON: Now look at the black-and-white version and you will see how far the two images are from one another.

COCTEAU: Yes. In black-and-white the preserved fruit, foetus-fruit, is much more akin to the real fruit lying on the table, but in color that on the table is far more fleshy or fleshlike. Those pieces are goddesses, compared to the ghosts in the jar.

ARAGON: The real point is that we suddenly understand how man has asserted his right to represent hitherto forbidden things.

COCTEAU: Here we have an ordinary object, magnified or glorified by the artist's calm confidence in his own genius, and a subconscious method of exercising it.

ARAGON: There is a kind of greatness or grandeur which does not exactly arise from the subject itself, and here we have an object that is absolutely characteristic of the age.

COCTEAU: Monet was a genius, innocent of pride, but so certain that he was a great painter that he could paint anything he wanted to.

ARAGON: Here we are at the hinge or turning-point between Impressionism and its aftermath.

COCTEAU: The "isthmuses."

ARAGON: The turning-point was that man, Monet, whom I met when he was still painting at Giverny. When I went back to look at his house not long ago I saw the relative poverty in which the Monet family are living now — a poverty with quite a lot of his paintings of water lilies lying about, marvels in that shabby squalor, everything in shabby squalor and shameful neglect.

COCTEAU: But why?

ARAGON: Because his estate had to be shared out after his death. It was an extraordinary upheaval. I've never seen anything so like Balzac, I mean his way of showing the breakdown of great families. Perhaps it concerns me because I used to live near there: I knew one of Monet's grandsons who looked like an Apache and used to paint batiks, things in fancywork. That was some thirty-three years ago. Only five or six years ago Elsa and I were looking at houses as we wanted to buy one, and that is how we saw the various properties of the Monet family. Way back in 1923 they were still the younger generation, but now they are as old as Monet was when I first went to Giverny. At that time Monet had a team of gardeners who had to pull up all the flowers in his garden every night so that he would never see a faded flower. He would go to sleep with a blue garden and wake up with a yellow one. Nothing but a shadow of all that is left, nothing but abject poverty and dreadful neglect. It is disgraceful that the French Government never took over those marvelous gardens with their water lilies — when one thinks of all the *Nymphéas* that Monet gave to France, why has France abandoned his living flowers?[21]

COCTEAU: There was a hard struggle to obtain some respect for Renoir's house. And it was the Americans who took up the Cézanne affair, thanks to the intervention of James Lord. But it's all over now, people don't give a damn any longer, they just let the curtain fall and let everything collapse offstage. All they care about is the fun and games on the radio. But we have to be fair, Louis: don't you think that Monet's wonderful glass jar, painted at a time when others were painting chunks of raw meat, is superior to all his water lilies and cathedrals? The water lilies and cathedrals have nothing like this controlled and mysterious energy.

ARAGON: But some of those things have a tremendous naturalness.

COCTEAU: Perhaps, but...

ARAGON: And you are less than fair to Monet's cathedrals.

COCTEAU: They could just as well be melting strawberry-ices. The phenomenon we are up against is the bogus realism of Monet and the Spanish painters. There is the object and its ghost, its spectral form. Monet's table is lyrical: it could just as well be a seething ocean, and the jar could be a Greek column, and the peaches could be goddesses.

ARAGON: Exactly. What has happened is that at one blow this jar has put an end to goddesses, the peaches have taken over in their own right. It could be said that with Monet's jar the whole of French painting at last asserts itself and takes over, so that people will no longer go to Flanders or Italy in pursuit of the mystery of color or of painting itself: from now on they will come to Paris, even if that annoys the entire world. And it is true that with Picasso and Matisse it has achieved throughout the world the importance it has today. But it all began with the Impressionists. There's no denying that it was in order to see Monet's work that they came over from America and Russia.

COCTEAU: You will remember how, when we were children, they used to drag us along to the Salon to look at the skivvies by a painter called Bail varnishing bottles and brasses. Bail's still lifes were well and truly still deaths: poor old Bail wasted all his skill and know-how on the "realism" of a dead window reflected in a dead jar.

ARAGON: Of course. You are interested in the abstractness of things, Jean; but what interests me is the particular sort of triumph thanks to which the phenomenon we saw in the fifteenth and sixteenth centuries, the pilgrimages that painters made, has now changed its center, so that what used to pass through Venice or Antwerp now passes through Paris.

COCTEAU: I should like to add how pleased I am that we can now talk about the enormous injustice done to Zola. Zola was a great lyric poet. He has not had the benefit of the distancing we have given the Impressionist painters. The injustice toward him is still going on. Many a chapter in Zola has the haunting beauty of Monet's jar.

ARAGON: It's not for me to contradict you. That lyricism of reality is surely the essence of French painting. And it is enduring, because even in Picasso — whom we have annexed for France — as you know, in Picasso there will suddenly appear a cork — for instance — that never existed two years before, one of those twisty corks in rubber or plastic. Or no matter what object, for Picasso sees things as they are entering life, and before the people who are using them and who don't even notice what they look like and are even a bit shamefaced and ready to hide them if anyone comments on them — such as that blue enamel pan, that new design of coffeepot... It is that power, that rare faculty of vision that is latent in a painting like this one before us. Monet saw his jar before anyone else. We have both been unwilling to end with this picture, we cannot finish with the one we care for most, but we have another masterpiece in reserve as a final tidbit.

COCTEAU: Unfortunately, greatness of soul has little to do with greatness of mind. They admired Zola's lyricism when it took the form of heroism during the Dreyfus affair. In my view his spiritual beauty shone out in the Dreyfus affair and that is what they deny in his books.

ARAGON: In any case, men like Zola represented the spirit of their age at its highest level. Of course there were certain limitations in his "slice of life," as they called it; but it was necessary to go through that in order to see beyond. Without that it would not have been possible to pass from romanticism into our own age, while in the field of ideas that isn't possible without passing through the phase of vision that we call naturalism, via Zola and the Impressionists. If we fail to understand and follow that path, then the generous ideas of our time, however great, remain incomprehensible and no better than rootless growths.

COCTEAU: We two have known, more than most people, the magnificent gangsters of Cubism, the knights of the Cubist tournament, dressed in corrugated iron and newsprint. I think that you who knew Monet will agree that before the Cubists came along there was a certain goodness and gentleness among artists. Monet's white beard evokes dear old Saint-Pol Roux, for me. He was a real Father Christmas. I met with the same kindness in Vuillard and Bonnard, both of them exquisite souls. We have lived through the age of violence. Our country cottage was a Martello tower, a stronghold. We had to defend ourselves against the bosses and the invading hordes.

ARAGON: You know, one odd thing is the kinship between Monet and another man, a poet: Monet had a Walt Whitman side to him.

COCTEAU: A royal comrade of flowers and sunshades. Whitman also had that legendary hyacinthine beard, those hairy antennae that grow from the heart... But let us now leave our bottled fuit and come to Van Gogh's splendid still life, the pears. Pears that only lie wounded and still have some life left in them, on the field of battle.

Vincent van Gogh
Still Life with Pears. Page 142

ARAGON: With this picture, which is just *Pears* and nothing else and which comes immediately after Monet's jar of peaches, we close a great epoch in our journey through the paintings in the Dresden collection, and in it we find a Dutch master of French painting. We find a Dutchman and the union is complete. On our way we have missed that international "marriage" in landscape, as almost the only landscape we had was Hobbema's, with little else until Monet, and we found no Jongkind on the way. But we have Van Gogh, and we could also have had his *Zouave* to place next to Renoir's captain. What we have here is his *Pears,* steeped in color.

Vincent van Gogh
The Zouave

COCTEAU: They are from the tree on which Van Gogh was crucified. He was the first martyr of that religion whose high priest was Picasso.

ARAGON: I must say that in ending with Van Gogh we are making amends for the chauvinism of what I said about French painting: first because Van Gogh's is no doubt French painting, but secondly because he helps us to pay our deep respects to the Dutch. We find them with us here in France, and we can see the unity that has been achieved from the late Middle Ages down to our own day in this sort of tour around European painting which, taking us from country to country, makes us return by way of Auvers-sur-Oise and yet still be in Leyden or Antwerp.

COCTEAU: And in those Elysian Fields where the heroes, drinking from the stream of oblivion, have forgotten their old struggles here on earth.

Appendix

Notes on the Dialogues

1 The Second World War exposed the Dresden Art Gallery to greater dangers than it had ever faced in its entire history. The gallery was closed in 1938 and 1939, even before the Nazi assault on Poland, and when the war with its horrors fell back on Germany itself, 1942 seeing the onset of ever more massive bomb attacks, the paintings were removed and taken to safety. Towards the end of the war, as the Soviet army moved closer, the paintings were removed from storage east of the Elbe and accommodated provisionally to the west of the river. However, the new storage space (for example the Cotta tunnel in the Rottwerndorf sandstone quarry near Pirna or the pit of the limestone quarry Pockau-Lengefeld near Marienberg) often put the pictures in jeopardy because of unfavorable climatic conditions.

On February 13, 1945, at a time when Hitler's defeat was already predictable, Dresden was destroyed. The 56 minutes of the two attacks reduced the inner part of the city almost completely to rubble and ashes. The Semper Gallery and the Zwinger were also severely damaged. When the Soviet army arrived in Dresden, the 164th battalion of the 5th guards' regiment of the 1st Ukrainian Front was charged with the recovery and removal to safety of the evacuated works of art. For years, while reconstruction began in Dresden, the paintings were housed in the museums of Moscow and Kiev. Soviet restorers preserved and treated those pictures which had suffered from the effects of enforced storage during the war.

On August 25, 1955, the Dresden paintings were handed over in Moscow to a government delegation from the German Democratic Republic. This official act marked the start of a new epoch in the history of the collection. While reconstruction work progressed on the first section of the building (the central part and east wing) until completion on May 15, 1956, the paintings were reintroduced to the public for the first time in 1955/56 in large special exhibitions at first in Moscow and then in Berlin. On June 3, 1956, the Dresden Art Gallery was reopened. The second stage of the reconstruction (the west wing and Deutscher Saal in the adjoining Zwinger Pavilion) was completed on October 4, 1960 — on the four hundredth anniversary of Dresden's state art collection.

2 By Vittore Carpaccio, Museo Civico, Venice.

3 National Museum, Warsaw.

4 More recent research rejects this interpretation. The sitter has been identified as Bernhard von Reesen.

5 Wrongly designated *fils* (son) in the original French text.

6 In the original text, wrongly named as *Jean le Bon*.

7 This canvas was by Jan Massys (also known as Matsys or Metsys) who painted in the Antwerp studio of his father, Quentin, who died in 1530.

8 The attribution of this work to Joos van Cleve (or Cleeve) is highly questionable. It is regarded as being the work of a German master of the sixteenth century.

9 Contrary to the original French edition of 1957, all the works discussed are now in color, with the exception of two pictures which because of prolonged restoration were not available in color: these were Cranach's *The Presentation in the Temple* and Joos van Cleve's *Descent from the Cross*. But in the case of pictures of which, for the purpose of emphasis in the discussions, reproductions in black-and-white were mentioned or compared with those in color, black-and-white illustrations have been added.

10 This painting is entitled *Chalking the Score in the Alehouse*.

11 In the original French text, Dresden is wrongly named instead of Delft.

12 There is certainly some misunderstanding here, as inquiry at the Museum of Modern Art shows that this work is not in their collection.

13 Footnote in the French edition: Some critics think that only the hand in this picture was painted by Velázquez himself.

14 Whereas the work of Fra Angelico (1387–1454) belongs to the first part of the fifteenth century, Aragon's remark refers to the second half of that century.

15 This interpretation of *A Lady in White* is incorrect and totally unacceptable. A painting bearing the inscription *Lavinia,* and which is a portrait of Titian's daughter, is in the Dresden Gallery (item 171).

16 Footnote in the French edition: The affair is much more complicated. Lucan wrote: *"A famulo Ganymede dolis pervenit ad hostes/ Caesaris Arsinoe quae castra carentia rege/ Ut proles Lagea tenet, famulumque Tyranni/ Terribilis justo transegit Achilles ferro."* This was put into French verse in about 1654 by M. de Marolles, the curious poet of the *Book of Painters and Engravers.* His rendering of Lucan has the advantage of adding details that were only hinted at in the original Latin: "Meanwhile Arsinoë, the king's younger sister, carried off from the palace by the wiles of the eunuch Ganymede, fled to the camp of Caesar's enemies in order to take command in Ptolemy's absence, being his nearest relation: she slew Achilles with her own hand after he revolted against the king and challenged her sovereignty." Thus we can see that this scene was not described in the *Pharsalia* and can be ascribed to Tintoretto's own imagination; while I cannot conceive that the knight whom we see here rescuing the naked women is the eunuch Ganymede, or that the artist was portraying a eunuch here. The context in the poem suggests that the building we see rising from the waves was the Palace of Pharos, according to de Marolles, who explains that "(Pharos) was an island in the sea when Proteus the Soothsayer ruled over Egypt; but it is now a strip of land reaching the walls of Alexandria." But when Brébeuf translated Lucan into French verse eighteen years later, he took Pharos to be the famous lighthouse at Alexandria, from which Arsinoë and her companion made their escape. After all, Ganymede could quite well have sent, either to the palace or the beacon, some brave young soldier less politically minded than himself, in his own place. All this would be quite beside the point, if it did not bring out Tintoretto's capacity for invention, which makes his picture far more than a mere illustration.

17 Footnote in the French edition: Here we have a curious color-blind fault of memory. Jean Cocteau, having imagined the wall in the Canaletto to be pink and then seeing the colored slide that confirmed his intuition, then imagined the wall was pink in Vermeer's *View of the Town of Delft* in the Hague Museum, though in fact it is yellow. In Proust's novel Bergotte died repeating "that little yellow wall."

18 Footnote in the French edition: In fact the canvas is regarded as having been painted by Poussin before leaving Paris, under the influence of the Chevalier Marini. But as it is loosely dated 1623–1626, this is far from certain. Poussin was in Rome from the beginning of 1624.

19 In the original French text, the titles of the two paintings have been mixed up; this one is entitled *A Love Festival.*

20 In the original French text, Cézanne is wrongly named instead of Van Gogh.

21 Claude Monet's house at Giverny was bequeathed to the Académie des Beaux-Arts by his son Michel. After careful restoration from 1977 onwards, it has been opened as a museum in 1980.

Notes on Works in the Dresden Gallery

CRANACH THE ELDER, LUCAS
Named after Kronach, his birthplace. Born there 1472, died in Weimar 1553. Active in Vienna, then from 1505 as court painter to the Electors of Saxony at Wittenberg. Journey to the Netherlands 1508. Founder of a school of far-reaching influence.

Portrait of Duke Henry the Pious
Painted in 1514, companion piece to no. 1906 H.
Transferred from limewood to canvas,
184 × 82.5.
Acquired for the Kunstkammer (art room) in 6141. Gal. no. 1906 G.

Portrait of Duchess Katharina of Mecklenburg
Consort of Duke Henry the Pious of Saxony.
Signed lower left with singed serpent, *LC*, and 1514. Companion piece to no. 1906 G.
Gal. no. 1906 H.

Adam
Signed lower left with winged serpent and 1531.
Companion piece to no. 1912.
Limewood, 170 × 69.5.
Acquired for the Kunstkammer in 1587.
Gal. no. 1911.

Eve
Companion piece to no. 1911.
Limewood, 169 × 69.
Provenance as with no. 1911. Gal. no. 1912.

The Earthly Paradise
Signed right (rock) with winged serpent and 1530.
Poplar, 80 × 117.
Acquired in 1928. Gal. no. 1908 A.

The St. Catherine Altarpiece, Left Panel
Center panel: the Martyrdom of Saint Catherine.
Left panel: Saints Dorothy, Agnes, and Cunegund.
Right panel: Saints Barbara, Ursula, and Margaret.
Center panel signed lower center: *LC* 1506.
Limewood, center panel 126 × 138, other panels 124 × 66.5 each.
Center and right panels figure in 1835 catalog; left panel acquired in 1946 from the Speck von Sternburg Collection at Lützschena. Gal. no. 1906 A, BB, B.

The Presentation in the Temple
Limewood, 83.5 × 120.
In the Kunstkammer since 1657.
After 1741 to the Gallery.
Gal. no. 1935.

DÜRER, ALBRECHT
Born in Nuremberg 1471, died there 1528.
First apprenticed in the goldsmith's shop of his father Albrecht Dürer. 1486—1490 pupil of Michael Wolgemut. 1490—1494 travel in the Upper Rhine. Active at Nuremberg from 1494 onwards. Journeys to Venice 1494/95 and 1505—1507. At Augsburg 1518. Journey to the Netherlands 1520/21.

Portrait of Bernhard von Reesen
(Portrait of a Young Man)
Signed upper center with monogram and 1521.
Oak, 45.5 × 31.5.
Probably acquired through Le Leu from Paris.
Gal. no. 1871.

The Dresden Altarpiece
Center panel: the Virgin worshiping her Child.
Left panel: Saint Anthony.
Right panel: Saint Sebastian.
Painted about 1496.
Tempera on canvas.
Center panel 117 × 96.5 (after patching), other panels 114 × 45.
In 1687 through Bottschild from the Castle Chapel in Wittenberg to the Kunstkammer.
Gal. no. 1869.

HOLBEIN THE YOUNGER, HANS
Born in Augsburg 1497, died in London 1543.
Pupil of his father Hans Holbein the Elder.
Active at Basel from 1515 onwards. At Lucerne 1517. Travels in France (1523 or 1524) and England (1526—1528) and probably Northern Italy. Active in London from 1532 onwards and from 1536 court painter to Henry VIII. Short stay at Basel in 1538.

Portrait of Charles de Solier, Sieur de Morette, French Ambassador to London
Painted 1534/35.
Resin tempera, oak, 92.5 × 75.
Acquired in 1746 from the Ducal Gallery at Modena as a Leonardo da Vinci (the sitter being assumed to be Ludovico Sforza).
Gal. no. 1890.

*Double Portrait of Sir Thomas Godsalve and
His Son John*
Dated upper left: Anno Dni. M. D. XXVIII.
Resin tempera, oak, 35 × 36.
Acquired in 1749 through Le Leu from Paris.
Gal. no. 1889.

DUTCH MASTER, ABOUT 1500

*The Holy Family in a Room with Joachim
and Anna*
Oak, 65.5 × 48.
Guarienti Inventory (1747–1750). Gal. no. 840.

EYCK, JAN VAN
Born in Maaseyck about 1390, died in Bruges
in 1441. Pupil of his brother Hubert van Eyck.
In 1425 court painter to Philip the Good in
Burgundy. Active at Bruges from 1431
onwards.

Triptych of the Virgin
Center panel: the Virgin and Child enthroned
in a church.
Inside left panel: the Archangel Michael
with kneeling donor.
Inside right panel: Saint Catherine.
Outside the panels: the Annunciation (in gray
monochrome).
Signed on foot of frame of center panel:
· *Johannes De eyck me fecit et complevit Anno
DM M'CCCC'XXXVII'· als· ixh· xan*
(Johannes van Eyck painted and completed
me AD 1437. As good as I can.)
Oak.
Center panel 33.1 × 27.5, other panels
33.1 × 13.6 each (glued framework included).
Inventory of 1754 as Albrecht Dürer.
Gal. no. 799.

MASSYS, JAN
Born in Antwerp about 1509, son of Quentin
Massys, and died there in 1575. From 1531
onwards, Master of the Guild at Antwerp.
In 1544 he was expelled for secretly being a
Protestant and probably went to France and
Italy. Active again in Antwerp from 1558
onwards.

The Moneylender and His Wife
Painted in 1539.
Oak, 85 × 115.
Acquired in 1749 from the Imperial Gallery,
Prague. Gal. no. 804.

CLEVE THE ELDER, JOOS VAN DER BEKE,
called VAN CLEVE
Born in Cleves or Antwerp about 1464, died
in Antwerp in 1540 or 1541. 1511, Master
of the St. Luke Guild at Antwerp. Travels to
Cologne, France, England, and Italy.

Portrait of a Beardless Man
Painted about 1513.
Oak, 42.5 × 30.5.
Inventory of 1722. Gal. no. 809 B.

CLEVE, JOOS VAN (?)/GERMAN MASTER,
SIXTEENTH CENTURY

Descent from the Cross
About 1510.
Oak, 87 × 69.
Acquired in 1874 from Fischer, Basel.
Gal. no. 1965.

BOL, HANS
Born in Mechlin 1534, died in Amsterdam
1593. Pupil of his uncle Jacob Bol. Among
other things he designed tapestries at
Mechlin. From 1574 to 1584 he was at
Antwerp, and from that time onwards
mainly at Amsterdam.

*Village Festival in Front of the Church
and Castle*
Signed lower left: Hans Bol 1582.
Parchment on oak, 14 × 21.
Kunstkammer Inventory of 1587. Gal. no. 823.

Jacob's Ladder
Parchment on oak, 14 × 21.5.
Kunstkammer Inventory of 1595. Gal. no. 828.

VALCKENBORCH, MAERTEN (I) VAN
Born in Louvain 1535, died in Frankfurt-am-
Main 1612. Member of the Guild at Mechlin
1559. Moved to Antwerp about 1565. In 1566
he left for Aix-la-Chapelle with his brother
Lucas and Hans Vredemann de Vries. Citizen
of Frankfurt-am-Main 1586.

The Tower of Babel
Signed bottom center:
*Martin van Valckenborch fecit et inventor
MVV 1595.*
Oak, 75.5 × 105.
Acquired in 1699 through Samuel Bottschild,
passed to the Kunstkammer 1700 and to the
Gallery after 1741. Gal. no. 832.

RUBENS, PETER PAUL
Born 1577 in Siegen, died in Antwerp 1640.
Pupil of Tobias Verhaecht, Adam van Noort,
and Otto van Veen at Antwerp. Was in Italy
from 1600 to 1608 (Venice, Mantua, Rome,
and Genoa). From late 1608 onwards he
painted chiefly at Antwerp. Journeys to Madrid

(1603/04 and 1628/29), to Paris (between 1621 and 1627), and London (1629/30).

Bathsheba at the Bath
Painted about 1635.
Oak, 175 × 126.
Acquired from Paris through Le Leu after 1749. Gal. no. 965.

Portrait of a Woman with Plaited Fair Hair
Oak, 64 × 49.5.
Acquired about 1747. Gal. no. 964 A.

DYCK, ANTHONIS VAN
Born in Antwerp 1599, died in London 1641. Pupil of Hendrik van Balen; assisted Peter Paul Rubens from 1616 onwards. Active at Antwerp, in London 1620/21, and in Italy from 1621 to 1627 mainly at Genoa. Court painter to Charles I in London from 1632 onwards.

Portrait of a Young Man
An early work.
Oak, 64 × 49.
Acquired in 1851 from Dr. Hille in Dresden. Gal. no. 1023 A.

BROUWER, ADRIAEN
Born probably in 1605 or 1606 in Oudenaarde in Flanders, died in Antwerp 1638. Pupil of Frans Hals in Haarlem from about 1624 onwards. Active 1625/26 in Amsterdam, then at Haarlem. At Antwerp from 1631 onwards.

Unpleasant Duties of a Father
Oak, 20 × 13.
Catalog of 1817. Gal. no. 1057.

OSTADE, ADRIAEN VAN
Born in Haarlem 1610, died there 1684. Pupil of Frans Hals, together with Adriaen Brouwer.

Peasants Carousing in an Inn
An early work.
Signed on seat, half-left: *Av. Ostade.*
Oak, 39 × 56.
Inventory of 1722. Gal. no. 1395.

HALS, JAN
Active in Haarlem about 1650. Pupil of his father Frans Hals.

Portrait of Frau Schmale
Signed: *Aet. suae 19, dat. 1644.*
Its companion piece signed "Jan Hals 1644," a portrait of Herr Schmale, was in a private Norwegian collection in 1930.
Canvas, 76 × 63.
Acquired in 1875 from Amsterdam art sale. Gal. no. 1361.

TENIERS THE YOUNGER, DAVID
Born in Antwerp 1610, died in Brussels 1690. Pupil of his father David Teniers the Elder. Master of the Guild at Antwerp from 1632.

Active at Antwerp. From 1651 onwards court painter and director of the gallery of Archduke Leopold Wilhelm at Brussels.

Fishermen on the Dunes
Signed: *D.T.F.*
Canvas, 83 × 119.
Inventory of 1722. Gal. no. 1069.

Chalking the Score in the Alehouse
Signed: *D. Teniers. F.*
Oak, 47 × 68.
Inventory of 1722: "From the Kunstkammer." Gal. no. 1073.

REMBRANDT, HARMENSZ. VAN RIJN
Born 1606 in Leyden, died in Amsterdam 1669. Pupil of Jacob van Swanenburgh at Leyden, and of Pieter Lastman at Amsterdam. Active at Leyden and Amsterdam from 1631 onwards.

The Falconer (Self-Portrait)
Signed upper left: *Rembrandt fe 1639.*
Oak, 121 × 89.
Guarienti Inventory (1747–1750). Gal. no. 1561.

Portrait of Saskia van Uijlenburgh as a Young Girl
Signed left: *Rembrandt. fe 1633.*
Oak, 52.5 × 44.5.
Catalog of 1817. Gal. no. 1556.

Saskia with a Red Flower
Signed lower left: *Rembrandt. f 1641.*
Oak, 98.5 × 82.5.
Acquired in 1742 from the Araignon Collection in Paris. Gal. no. 1562.

Ganymede in the Eagle's Talons
(The Rape of Ganymede)
Signed on shirttail: *Rembrandt. fe 1635.*
Canvas, 171 × 130.
Acquired in 1751 through von Heinecken from Hamburg.
Gal. no. 1558.

VERMEER VAN DELFT, JAN
Born in Delft 1632, died there 1675. Pupil of Carel Fabritius. Member of the Guild at Delft in 1653. Active also as an art dealer.

Girl Reading a Letter
Only traces of former signature, center right, no longer intelligible.
Painted about 1659.
Canvas, 83 × 64.5.
Acquired in 1742 through de Brais from Paris. Gal. no. 1336.

Matchmaking
(The Procuress?)
Signed lower right: *J V Meer: 1656.*
Canvas, 143 × 130.
Acquired in 1741 from the Wallenstein Collection at Dux.
Gal. no. 1335.

HOBBEMA, MEINDERT
Born in Amsterdam 1638, died there 1709. Pupil of Jacob van Ruisdael. Active at Amsterdam, where he held the municipal office of gauger of wine and oil from 1668 onwards.

The Water-Mill
Signed lower center: *M Hobbema.*
Oak, 59.5 × 84.5.
Acquired in 1899 at the Schubart auction in Munich. Gal. no. 1664 A.

RUISDAEL, JACOB ISAACKSZ. VAN
Born in Haarlem about 1628/29, died there 1682. Pupil of his uncle Salomon van Ruysdael. Removal to Amsterdam 1656 or 1657, where he worked later as a physician after taking a doctor's degree in medicine at Caen in 1676.

The Jewish Cemetery near Ouderkerk
Signed lower left: *J v Ruisdael.*
Painted after 1670.
Canvas, 84 × 95.
Inventory of 1754. Gal. no. 1502.

REYNOLDS, SIR JOSHUA
Born in Plympton 1723, died in London 1792. Pupil of Thomas Hudson. Influenced by the Italians and by Van Dyck and Rembrandt. Worked as a portrait-painter in London. In Italy from 1750 to 1752. Became first President of the Royal Academy in London in 1768.

Portrait of Mr. William James in the Costume of the Dunstable Hunt
Painted in 1758.
Canvas, 111 × 89.
Acquired in 1891 from Berlin art sale.
Gal. no. 798 C.

ENGLISH SCHOOL

GRECO, DOMENIKOS THEOTOKOPOULOS,
known as EL GRECO (the Greek)
Born in Fódele in Crete 1541, died in Toledo 1614. Pupil of Titian in Venice after 1566, influenced by Tintoretto and Michelangelo. At Rome 1570, active in Toledo from 1577 onwards.

Christ Healing the Blind Man
An early (Venetian) work by the artist.
Poplar, 65.5 × 84.
Acquired in 1741 through Ventura Rossi from Venice. Gal. no. 276.

RIBERA, JUSEPE DE,
known as LO SPAGNOLETTO
Born in Játiva near Valencia 1591, died in Naples 1652. Pupil of Francisco Ribalta at Valencia, developed his style in Italy. Active at Naples from 1616 onwards.

Saint Agnes in Prison
Signed lower center: *Jusepe de Ribera español, F. 1641.*
Canvas, 203 × 152.
Acquired in 1745 through Count de Bene de Masseran. Gal. no. 683.

VELÁZQUEZ, DIEGO RODRIGUEZ DE SILVA Y
Born in Seville 1599, died in Madrid 1660. Pupil of Francisco Herrera the Elder and Francisco Pacheco at Seville. Court painter to Philip IV in Madrid from 1623 onwards. Stayed in Italy from 1629 to 1631 and from 1649 to 1651.

Portrait of Gaspar de Guzmán, Count Olivares, Minister to Philip IV
Painted in the artist's studio.
Canvas, 92.5 × 74.
Acquired in 1746 from the Ducal Gallery at Modena. Gal. no. 699.

Portrait of Gaspar de Guzmán
Detail of hand.

Portrait of a Gentleman,
probably Juan Mateos, Master of the Royal Staghounds
Painted about 1631/32.
Canvas, 108.5 × 90.
Acquired in 1746 from the Ducal Gallery at Modena as a Rubens. Gal. no. 697.

ZURBARÁN, FRANCISCO DE
Born in Fuente de Cantos 1598, died in Madrid 1664. Pupil of Pedro Diaz de Villanueva in Seville. Active in Madrid and Seville and appointed municipal painter there in 1629.

St. Bonaventura Praying
(Theobald Visconti elected Pope Gregory X, 1271)
Painted in 1629.
Canvas, 238 × 222.
Acquired in 1853 from the Louis-Philippe Collection, London. Gal. no. 696.

SPANISH SCHOOL

ITALIAN SCHOOL

FRA ANGELICO, SCHOOL OF (1837–1455)

The Annunciation
Tempera on poplar, 27 × 44.
Acquired in 1846 from the Rumohr sale.
Gal. no. 7.

PINTURICCHIO, BERNARDINO DI BETTO BIAGIO, known as PINTURICCHIO
Born in Perugia about 1454, died in Siena 1513.
Pupil of Fiorenzo di Lorenzo, assistant to
Perugino in Rome. Active in Perugia, Rome,
Orvieto, and at Siena from 1503 onwards.

Portrait of a Boy
Probably painted between 1481 and 1483.
Tempera on poplar, 50 × 35.5.
Inventory of 1722 listed as a portrait of
Raphael. Gal. no. 41.

BELLINI, SCHOOL OF GIOVANNI
(about 1430–1516, Venice)

The Virgin with the Body of Christ
A free reproduction of an early composition
by Giovanni Bellini.
Tempera on poplar, 56.5 × 38.5.
Bequeathed in 1892 by Mr. and Mrs.
G. W. E. J. Kestner in Dresden. Gal. no. 52 A.

GIORGIONE, GIORGIO DA CASTELFRANCO, known as GIORGIONE
Born in Castelfranco about 1477, died in
Venice 1510. Together with Titian a pupil
of Giovanni Bellini in Venice. Active in
Venice.

Venus Asleep
After the master's death, finished by Titian.
Canvas, 108 × 175.
Acquired in 1699 through C. le Roy. Gal. no. 185.

PALMA VECCHIO, JACOPO D'ANTONIO DE NEGRETI, known as PALMA VECCHIO
Born in Serinalta near Bergamo about 1480,
died in Venice 1528. Pupil of Giovanni Bellini
and influenced by Giorgione and Titian.
Active mainly in Venice.

Venus Reposing
From the artist's middle period.
Canvas, 112 × 186.
Acquired from Italy in 1728. Gal. no. 190.

Jacob and Rachel
Later period.
Canvas, 146 × 250.
Guarienti Inventory (1747–1750) listed as
Giorgione from the Casa Malipiero in Venice.
Gal. no. 192.

TITIAN, TIZIANO VECELLIO, known as TITIAN
Born in Pieve di Cadore in 1477 or later, died
in Venice 1576. Pupil of Giovanni Bellini. Style
influenced by Giorgione. Active mainly in

Venice. In Padua 1511, Rome 1545/46, and
Augsburg 1548 and 1550/51.

Portrait of a Lady in White
Probably painted about 1555.
Canvas, 102 × 86.
Acquired in 1746 from the Ducal Gallery,
Modena. Gal. no. 170.

TINTORETTO, JACOPO ROBUSTI, known as TINTORETTO
Born in Venice 1518, died there 1594. A pupil
of Titian, strongly influenced by the work
of Michelangelo.

The Deliverance of Arsinoë
Probably painted soon after 1560.
Canvas, 153 × 251.
Acquired in 1743 through Algarotti from
Mantua. Gal. no. 269.

Portrait of an Old and a Young Man
Canvas, 99.5 × 121.
Acquired in 1749 from the Imperial Gallery,
Prague. Gal. no. 270.

PIAZZETTA, GIOVANNI BATTISTA
Born in Venice 1683, died there 1754. Pupil
of Antonio Molinari in Venice and Giuseppe
Maria Crespi in Bologna. Active mainly in
Venice.

A Young Standard-Bearer
Painted 1620–25.
Canvas, 87 × 71.5.
Acquired in 1743 through Algarotti from
Venice. Gal. no. 571.

TIEPOLO, GIOVANNI BATTISTA
Born in Venice 1696, died in Madrid 1770.
Pupil of Gregorio Lazzarini in Venice.
Influenced by Sebastiano Ricci, Piazzetta,
and Veronese. Active in Venice and region,
in Milan, Würzburg (1750–53), and from 1762
onwards in Madrid.

The Triumph of Amphitrite
Belongs to a series representing the four
elements, painted by Tiepolo about 1740 for
the entrance-hall of a Venetian palace.
Canvas, 213 × 442.
Acquired in 1927. Gal. no. 580 B.

GUARDI, FRANCESCO
Born in Venice 1712, died there 1793.
Influenced by Antonio Canal and Marco Ricci.
Active mainly in Venice.

*Pope Pius VI Blessing the Venetians
from the Scuola di San Marco* (1782)
Canvas, 51.5 × 68.
Acquired in 1898 from London art sale.
Gal. no. 601 A.

156

CANALETTO, GIOVANNI ANTONIO CANAL,
known as CANALETTO
Born 1697 in Venice, died there 1768. Pupil
of his father Bernardo Canal; influenced by
Luca Carlevarijs. Active mainly in Venice,
1746–1756 with short absences in England.

*The Piazza in Front of San Giacomo
di Rialto in Venice*
Painted shortly before 1730.
Canvas, 95.5 × 117.
Inventory of 1754. Gal. no. 583.

BELLOTTO, BERNARDO, known as CANALETTO
Born 1721 in Venice, died in Warsaw 1780.

Nephew and pupil of Antonio Canal. Painted
first in Italy; at Dresden 1747–1758, from
1748 onwards court painter to Augustus III;
in Vienna 1759/60, Munich 1761, return to
Dresden, from 1764 taught at Dresden
Academy. From 1767 onwards in Warsaw;
1768 court painter to Stanislas Augustus
Poniatowski, King of Poland.

The Neustädter Market in Dresden
Painted in 1750.
Canvas, 134 × 236.
In 1751 given to the Gallery by the artist him-
self. Gal. no. 612.

POUSSIN, NICOLAS
Born 1594 in Villers, died in Rome 1665.
Pupil of Quentin Varin. From 1612 in Paris;
style influenced by Ferdinand Elle and
Georges Lallemand. From 1624 in Rome;
development influenced by classical antiquity,
Raphael, Titian, Annibale Carracci,
Domenichino. 1641/42 temporary stay in Paris.

Narcissus
Painted in the artist's early Roman phase.
Canvas, 72 × 96.5.
Acquired through Le Plat in 1725. Gal. no. 722.

LORRAIN OR LE LORRAIN, CLAUDE GELLÉE,
known as CLAUDE LORRAIN
Born 1600 in Chamagne in Lorraine, died in
Rome 1682. Pupil of Agostino Tassi in Rome;
influenced by Annibale Carracci, Paul Bril,
Adam Elsheimer, and Nicolas Poussin. In
Rome from about 1613 onwards.

Coast Scene with Acis and Galatea
Signed lower right: *CLAUDE GELLE IVEF
ROMA 1657.*
Canvas, 100 × 135.
Inventory of 1754. Gal. no. 731.

WATTEAU, ANTOINE
Born in Valenciennes 1684, died in Nogent near
Vincennes 1721. Pupil of Claude Gillot and
Claude Audran. Active mainly in Paris.

A Garden Party
A late work.
Canvas, 60 × 75.
Guarienti Inventory (1747–1750). Gal. no. 781.

LA TOUR, MAURICE QUENTIN DE
Born in Saint-Quentin 1704, died there 1788.
Self-taught pastelist. Active in Paris.

Count Maurice of Saxony, Marshal of France
(Le Maréchal de Saxe)
Paper, 59.5 × 49.
Catalog of 1765. Gal. no. P 164.

LIOTARD, JEAN-ETIENNE
Born in Geneva 1702, died there 1789. Pupil
of Daniel Gardelle, Jean-Baptiste Massé,
and François Le Moine in Paris. Active in
Rome 1736, Constantinople 1738–1742, then
in Vienna, Venice, Darmstadt, Lyons,
Geneva, Paris, London, Amsterdam. From 1758
onwards lived in Geneva.

The Chocolate-Girl
Pastel, executed in Vienna between 1743 and
1745.
Parchment, 82.5 × 52.5.
Acquired in 1745 through Algarotti from
Venice. Gal. no. P 161.

Self-Portrait in Turkish Costume
Paper, 60.5 × 46.5.
Catalog of 1765, supposedly acquired in 1747
through the Duke of Richelieu.
Gal. no. P 159.

MANET, EDOUARD
Born in Paris 1832, died there 1883. After a
voyage to Brazil as an apprentice where he
filled his logbook with drawings, entered
Thomas Couture's studio in 1850. Travels in
Italy (1853 and 1856), Holland, Germany,
Austria (1856), and Spain (1865). The
realistic elements in his work caused an open
scandal with the exhibition of such canvases
as the *Déjeuner sur l'herbe* (Open-Air Lunch;
1863) and *Olympia* (1865). Manet, who first
learnt from the great Spanish masters of the
seventeenth century, then Delacroix,
continued to follow his own inclinations and
after 1870 turned towards Impressionist
techniques without completely belonging to the
movement.

Lady in a Pink Dress
(Madame Marlin), 1881.
Signed lower left: *Manet.*
Canvas, 94 × 75.
Acquired in 1921 from the A. Rothermundt
Collection, Dresden. Gal. no. 2598.

FRENCH SCHOOL

DEGAS, HILAIRE GERMAIN EDGAR
Born 1834 in Paris, died there 1917. 1855 pupil
of L. Lamothe, Ecole des Beaux-Arts in
Paris. 1873 traveled in North America, and
1880 in Spain. 1874 exhibited in the first
Impressionist exhibition in Paris and also took
part in those that followed.

Lady with Binoculars
Signed lower right: *Degas* (in white), *Degas*
(ochre).
Pasteboard, 48 × 32.
Acquired in 1922 from the W. von Seidlitz
Collection (exchange). Gal. no. 2601.

Two Dancers
About 1898.
Signed lower right: *Degas.*
Pastel on paper, 95.5 × 87.
Acquired in 1919 from Berlin art sale
(exchange). Gal. no. 2586.

TOULOUSE-LAUTREC, HENRI RAYMOND DE
Born 1864 in Albi, died 1901 in Château
de Malromé. In Paris 1883/84 pupil of
L. Bonnat and F. Cormon.

Two Women-Friends
Signed lower left: *HTL-autrec* (ligated) *1895.*
Pasteboard on mahogany, 81.5 × 59.5.
Acquired in 1925 from Berlin art sale.
Gal. no. 3887.

GAUGUIN, PAUL
Born in Paris 1848, died 1903 in Atuana,
Marquesas Islands. Self-taught, began painting
in 1875. Stimulated by travels in Brittany
(1886) and Panama and Martinique (1887),
reacted against Impressionism. 1891 traveled
to Polynesia where he settled finally after 1896.

Two Tahitian Women
1892.
Signed lower right: *Para Api P Gauguin 92.*
Canvas, 67 × 92.
Acquired in 1926 from a Copenhagen private
collection at the International Art Exhibition,
Dresden. Gal. no. 2610.

RENOIR, AUGUSTE
Born in Limoges 1841, died in Cagnes,
Provence, in 1919. Trained as a decorator of
porcelain, ceramics, and fans, Renoir came
to Charles Gleyre's studio in Paris in 1862,
where he met Sisley, Monet and J. F. Bazille.

After meeting V. Diaz and Cézanne he became
acquainted with Courbet in 1868 and was
strongly influenced by him. After 1879 travel
and study in Algeria, Italy, Spain, Holland,
England, and 1910 in Munich.

Portrait of Captain Darras
1871.
Signed lower left: *Renoir 71.*
Canvas, 81 × 65.
Acquired in 1926 from a Dresden private
collection at the International Art Exhibition,
Dresden. Gal. no. 2608.

MONET, CLAUDE
Born in Paris 1840, died in Giverny 1926.
Studied in Paris with Pissarro in the *Académie
suisse.* 1862 active in Charles Gleyre's studio
where he met Renoir, Sisley, Bazille, Courbet,
and Manet. From 1871 onwards travels in
Holland, London, etc., then (again) settled
at Argenteuil. In 1874 Monet exhibited in the
first Impressionist Exhibition his *Impression,
soleil levant* (Impression of Sunrise) with the
result that he and his friends were nicknamed
Impressionists.

A Bend in the Seine near Lavacourt
1879.
Signed lower left: *Claude Monet.*
Canvas, 65.6 × 80.
Acquired in 1909 from Paris art sale.
Gal. no. 2525 A.

Still Life with Peaches
(The Jar of Peaches)
Signed lower right: *Claude Monet.*
Canvas, 55.5 × 46.
Acquired in 1927 from Berlin art sale.
Gal. no. 2525 B.

GOGH, VINCENT VAN
Born 1853 in Groot Zundert, Holland, died
1890 in Auvers-sur-Oise, France. During his
stay in Paris (1886—1888) associated with the
French Impressionist painters. 1889 admitted
to the mental hospital at Saint-Rémy.

Still Life with Pears
(Quinces), 1888/89.
Painted in Arles between February 21, 1888
and May 8, 1889.
Canvas, 46 × 59.5.
Acquired in 1920 from Berlin art sale (exchange).
Gal. no. 2593

Illustrations Given for Comparison

This appendix offers a selection of the most important works from other collections mentioned in the dialogues.

BOTTICELLI, SANDRO

1 Botticelli, Sandro, properly named Alessandro Filipepi
Primavera.
Wood, 203 × 314. Uffizi, Florence.

BRUEGHEL THE ELDER, PIETER

2 Brueghel, the Elder, Pieter
The Tower of Babel.
Wood, 114 × 155. Kunsthistorisches Museum, Vienna.

CÉZANNE, PAUL

3 Cézanne, Paul
Women Bathing.
Canvas. Louvre (Musée du Jeu de Paume), Paris.

CLEVE THE ELDER, JOOS VAN

4 Cleve the Elder, Joos van
The Death of Mary.
Wood, 127 × 154. Alte Pinakothek, Munich.

CRANACH THE ELDER, LUCAS

5 Cranach the Elder, Lucas
Spring Nymph.
Wood, 59 × 91.5. Museum der bildenden
Künste, Leipzig.

DAVID, JACQUES-LOUIS

6 David, Jacques-Louis
The Death of Marat.
Canvas, 165 × 128. Musées Royaux des Beaux-
Arts, Brussels.

DELAUNAY, ROBERT

7 Delaunay, Robert
The Red Eiffel Tower.
Canvas, 126 × 54. Guggenheim Museum,
New York.

160

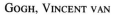

GOGH, VINCENT VAN

8 Gogh, Vincent van
The Zouave.
Canvas, 65 × 54. Stedelijk Museum, Amsterdam.

GOYA, FRANCISCO JOSÉ DE

9 Goya, Francisco José de
The Family of Charles IV.
Canvas, 280 × 336. Prado, Madrid.

10 Goya, Francisco José de
The Milkmaid.
Canvas, 68 × 50.5. Fine Arts Museum, Budapest.

GRECO, EL

11 Greco, Domenikos Theotokopoulos,
known as El Greco
Portrait of Giulio Clovio.
Canvas, 65 × 95. Museo di Capodimonte,
Naples.

12 Greco, Domenikos Theotokopoulos,
known as El Greco
Youth Blowing on Charcoal.
Canvas, 65 × 50. Museo di Capodimonte,
Naples.

13 Greco, Domenikos Theotokopoulos,
known as El Greco
The Burial of Count Orgaz.
Canvas, 480 × 360. St. Tomé, Toledo.

GUARDI, FRANCESCO

14 Guardi, Francesco
Pope Pius VI Blessing the Crowd in the Piazza
in Front of St. John and St. Paul.
Canvas, 63 × 80. Ashmolean Museum, Oxford.

HOBBEMA, MEINDERT

15 Hobbema, Meindert
The Avenue at Middelharnis.
Canvas, 103.5 × 141. National Gallery, London.

162

16 Manet, Edouard
The Fife Player.
Canvas, 161 × 97. Louvre, Paris.

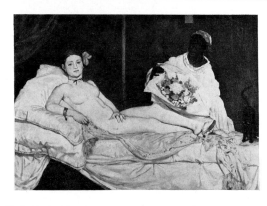

17 Manet, Edouard
Olympia.
Canvas, 130 × 190. Louvre, Paris.

MATISSE, HENRI

18 Matisse, Henri
The Dance.
Canvas, 260 × 391. Hermitage Museum,
Leningrad.

PICASSO, PABLO

19 Picasso, Pablo
War and Peace.
Fiber board, 470 × 1020 each. Vallauris,
Chapelle du Château.

20 Poussin, Nicolas
Acis and Galatea.
Canvas, Prado, Madrid.

RENOIR, AUGUSTE

21 Renoir, Auguste
Portrait of Madame Samary.
Canvas, 173 × 103. Hermitage Museum,
Leningrad.

TITIAN

22 Titian, properly named Tiziano Vecellio
Perseus and Andromeda.
Canvas, 179 × 197. Wallace Collection, London.

23 Titian, properly named Tiziano Vecellio
Reclining Venus.
Canvas, 119 × 165. Uffizi, Florence.

24 Velázquez, Diego Rodriguez de Silva y
The Surrender of Breda.
Canvas, 307 × 367. Prado, Madrid.

VERMEER VAN DELFT, JAN

25 Vermeer van Delft, Jan
View of the Town of Delft.
Canvas, 89.5 × 117.5. Mauritshuis, The Hague.

26 Vermeer van Delft, Jan
Girl with a Turban.
Canvas, 46.5 × 40. Mauritshuis, The Hague.

27 Vermeer van Delft, Jan
Allegory of the Artist (The Studio).
Canvas, 120 × 100. Kunsthistorisches Museum,
Vienna

WATTEAU, ANTOINE

28 Watteau, Antoine
The Art Dealer Gersaint's Signboard
Canvas, 182 × 308. Charlottenburg Castle,
Berlin (West)

29 Watteau, Antoine
The Bivouac.
Canvas, 32 × 45. Pushkin Museum, Moscow

Acknowledgments
Figures in roman type are page numbers
and indicate plates in the main text; those
in italics refer to plates in the Appendix.

Ashmolean Museum, Oxford *14*
Charlottenburg Castle, Berlin (West) *28*
Deutsche Fotothek, Dresden 38, 55, 116
Documentation photographique de la Réunion
   des musées nationaux, Paris *3, 16, 17*
Éditions Cercle d'Art, Paris *19*
Fine Arts Museum, Budapest *10*
Guggenheim Museum, New York *7*
Hermitage Museum, Leningrad *18, 21*
Kunsthistorisches Museum, Vienna *2, 27*
M. A. S., Barcelona *13*
Mauritshuis, The Hague *25, 26*
Musées Royaux des Beaux-Arts, Brussels *6*

Museo di Capodimonte, Naples *11, 12*
Museum der bildenden Künste, Leipzig *5*
National Gallery, London *15*
Prado, Madrid *9, 20, 24*
Publisher's Archives 52, 53, 73 bottom, 87,
   93, 113, 115, 118 bottom, 131, 138 bottom,
   139, 140, 141 right, *29*
Gerhard Reinhold, Mölkau near Leipzig 33, 34,
   35, 36, 37, 39, 40, 41, 42, 51, 53, 54, 56, 57,
   58, 59, 60, 61, 62, 63, 64, 65, 66, 67, 68, 69,
   73 top, 74, 88, 89, 91, 92, 94, 108, 110, 111,
   112, 114, 117, 118 top, 119, 120, 121, 122, 132,
   133, 134, 135, 136, 137, 138 top, 141 left, 142
Scala, Florence *1, 4, 23*
Stedelijk Museum, Amsterdam *8*
Verlag der Kunst, Dresden/Beyer 70, 72, 90,
   107, 109
Wallace Collection, London *22*